In Search of
The Lionheart Nation

by
Martin Walker

**Grosvenor House
Publishing Limited**

This book is published by
Grosvenor House Publishing Ltd
28-30 High Street, Guildford, Surrey, GU1 3EL.
www.grosvenorhousepublishing.co.uk

A CIP record for this book
is available from the British Library

ISBN 978-1-78148-815-7

Dedicated to my beautiful daughter Hannah
who will never know how much I love her

This royal throne of kings, this sceptred isle,
This earth of majesty, this seat of Mars,
This other Eden, demi-paradise;
This fortress, built by nature for herself,
Against infection, and the hand of war;
This happy breed of men, this little world;
This precious stone set in the silver sea,
Which serves it in the office of a wall,
Or as a moat defensive to a house,
Against the envy of less happier lands;
This blessed plot, this earth, this realm, this England,
This nurse, this teeming womb of royal kings,
Fear'd by their breed, and famous by their birth,
Renowned for their deeds as far from home
(For Christian service and true chivalry)
As is the sepulchre, in stubborn Jewry,
Of the world's ransom, blessed Mary's Son;
This land of such dear souls, this dear, dear land,
Dear for her reputation through the world,
Is now leas'd out, - I die pronouncing it, -
Like to a tenement, or pelting farm:
England, bound in with the triumphant sea,
Whose rocky shore beats back the envious siege
Of watr'y Neptune, is now bound in with shame,
With inky blots, and rotten parchment bonds:
That England, that was wont to conquer others,
Hath made a shameful conquest of itself.

William Shakespeare

v

Contents

Preface

I have often lamented the passing of our glorious leaders of history, their absence never invoked such profound nostalgia as now felt in the nation we call England today. Thus who is left to be inspired by? Who now carries the flag of this once great nation? The truth is, when England's back is against the wall, in times of trying conflict, great leaders of men have emerged and stood tall in the face of adversity. Against surmounting odds, they prevailed. Their valour, devotion and influence of the past have given rise to our unique identity - an identity now challenged on a daily basis. The purpose of this research is to inspire and reignite passion and pride, long bereft in our postmodern ranks, and to stand defiantly against those who see our history less favourably.

In the process of writing this book I have conceded numerous debts of gratitude which is a pleasure to acknowledge. I have found it virtually impossible to claim any expertise on such a rich and satisfying topic, myself in the process becoming very aware of the dependency on the labours of other scholars who have done the ground research. My biggest debt therefore goes to all whose writings I have plundered, and with crediting them unreservedly, I hope they forgive any misuse. In recognising their contribution, I sincerely thank them. While in attempting to create an individual and original piece of writing, I acknowledge the experts would probably find nothing new. However, it was written with the ambition of reaching out to the average person, or at least those who have an interest in English history and the characters that curiously shaped it. My own reflections suggest that it is the common person who embodies that elusive Englishness the most - that Englishness which our great leaders have so much influenced throughout the centuries. Indeed, this book hopes to explore and invite the reader to rediscover that all too frequently subverted identity that was once immutable. An identity often subverted unfortunately through fear of offending in one way or another, as England's presence or Englishness is so often a source of irritation or aggravation of some kind. I have tried to keep this a factual account of 'our island story', bound by 'its private language and its common memories'. It looks at our national history in search of inspiration and encouragement, often emanating from some of our greatest leaders. When writing about such men, I have noticed a tendency to exaggerate their importance as individuals and consequently neglect a wider appreciation for the times and circumstances surrounding them. I am guilty as charged of this offence, but feel further compelled to say that while attempting to argue objectively, it remains difficult to overstate the impact of their contribution to the course of history. This was intended as a celebration of English history and shall not dwell on the cancer of political correctness. Unfortunately as a writer, it seems to me impossible to avoid error, of being accused of wrong-headedness or belonging to some school of thought. So be it. A man can only face one direction. The Literary theorists can judge what they will.

The Shakespearean quote at the beginning of this book generates a romantic image of an England which many choose to reject. 'This England' as a 'sceptred isle' has many enemies old and new, from within and without. I remember once, during my university days, reading a book called *The English Nation – The Great Myth*, by Edwin Jones. Though robustly well written, it implied that English history as commonly told is largely a fabrication of our own self-indulgence; that we should look back in shame and look forward to a future where our only salvation lies in Europe. My less than appreciative reaction is also another motivation for writing this book. People seem less enthralled to write about English history, not simply because of the over-exaggerated method of historiography, but also because we have been persuaded through lack of confidence that we don't have much to celebrate. Of course Britain is no longer a world superpower. I for one believe that our contemporary situation is now dubious, however, our narrative cannot just be told as one of increasing decline. Our identity is clearly threatened and on the ropes, but collectively, on these occasions, we are able to punch well above our weight. We must remember our history, not dismiss it. Our glorious past should be sung of, not twisted into Anglophobic propaganda. The England of our imagination, elusive as it may seem, can still flourish. George Orwell once wrote that despite our lack of intelligence and artistic flair, our hypocritical attitude towards the empire and our lack of efficiency, 'in moments of supreme crisis the whole nation can suddenly draw together and act upon a species of instinct, really a code of conduct understood by almost everyone, though never formulated'. Though we may be embarking on an identity crisis now, it is my sincere hope that all readers will enjoy and find inspiration from engaging with the following pages. In adopting this concise structure, I concede that much has had to be left out and some areas only touched upon. I also accept that the content in these pages may appear to be of an insular nature to some, particularly when glossing over patriotism and nationalism; but I beseech the reader, British people are in no way insular in the way that they are often accused; Brits have had more contact with the outside world than any other nation.

I admit, much of that contact with other cultures has been of an aggressive and confrontational nature, however, I implore the reader to bear in mind that England has been compelled to largely define itself through fighting. Confrontation is mostly all England has ever known, and, as Linda Colley revealed: 'If a recent trans-European survey is correct, over two thirds of Britons remain only too willing to fight for their country. By contrast, less than half of their European neighbours indicate a similar willingness to express their patriotism in this fashion'. Re-evaluating the turmoil of our rich ancestral heritage will shed light on this national characteristic, a trait which was not formed by accident but through a tumultuous fusion of nature and nurture over centuries of survival.

We are entering testing times. England has been a punch bag for far too long over recent years. It needs to stand tall as it rightfully should. With the benefit of hindsight, the following pages amidst the first chapter reflect the ambivalent feelings that England has of itself. I have exercised restrain in advocating what many would feel to be an insulating type of individualism or separatism but the fear of being rootless, however, bubbles to the surface in an intermitted fashion yet hopefully offers some rudimental and incandescent clarity. The scarcity of detailing Wales, Scotland or Ireland is deliberate but meant with no disrespect. This is an enquiry into English identity, and, Welsh, Scottish and Irish writers will endeavour to investigate their own respective identities. With Scotland questioning its union with England and contemplating a private relationship with Europe, Ireland already bullied into joining Europe, it is almost time for England to look deep within itself. For such a critically important decision as to whether England should commit further to Europe, England's historical identity and deep cultural roots will be a vital factor in arriving at a decision. It will not be economics or party politics but a deeper consideration of our historical identity and core values that will influence our reasoning. This book is not intended as an exercise of self-flagellation; however, I leave you here with one thought: a nation that forgets its past has no foundation for the future.

CHAPTER 1

Introduction

People say you're born innocent, but it's not true.
You inherit all kinds of things that you can do
nothing about. You inherit your identity, your
history, like a birthmark that you can't wash
off...We are born with our heads turned back

(Hugo Hamilton)

National passions are rooted in images which
run back through hundreds of years. ...Yet they
dominate our lives...These collective memories,
whether imposed from above as ruling ideologies
or forged from below by the struggle of emerging
social movements, are the means whereby we
remember the past, our history, and therefore
they both guide our present actions and shape
our futures

(Steven Rose)

Engaging with history puts us in touch with our
ancestral roots, our very sense of identity. Knowledge
and awareness of what happened in the past, is a vital
factor for guidance in the future. Our psychological

stability depends on a firm sense of belonging; a belonging synchronised to a nation's collective memory thus situating our sense of identity in connection with a particular society or community. Such communities have an unprecedented impact in cultivating our values and attitudes towards the 'other'. This process seems to be external as well as internal with the 'other' projecting its own version of reality. The identification of a nation-state works in much the same way. It embodies its people's essence; the collective spirit of its inhabitants. Our identity then is perhaps something tangible or even organically connected as opposed to being abstract or metaphysical. It remains quite difficult not to identify with a nation-state in one form or another. The international Passport system clearly states your nationality thus officiating your identity for the world to see. However, identity shared collectively on a coherent national basis was not always so prevalent as it has been for the last six hundred years or so. These pages attempt to retrace England's steps back to the beginning to where the concept of Englishness and what constitutes being English were first formulated. Along the way, this concise book attempts to consider some of the greatest leaders to have influenced the English identity and to cast a fleeting gaze into England's future and her immediate existential concerns.

At the close of the nineteenth century and dawn of the twentieth century, Britain was categorically the greatest imperial power in the world; with key strategic territories around the globe maintained and serviced by an unrivalled navy, the sun never setting on history's greatest empire. The discovery and acquisition of America situated Britain at the epicentre of the new world as opposed to 'being on the edge of the old world'. Becoming the dominant trading and colonising nation added to the idea of an English legacy of a unique and continuous story of conquest and achievement. By 1919, the year of the Paris Peace Treaty, Britain was at her greatest. She had the largest navy in history with 33 cruisers, 36 battleships, 8 battle cruisers and over a hundred destroyers. Such a Navy was purposely constructed to be numerically superior to any competitive fleets. Almost a million miles of the Turkish and German empires had been taken, placing her protectorate over a combined 450 million souls spreading over a quarter of the earth's surface. Whatever the conditions in their home country, all were free to enter the United Kingdom at will. The downward trajectory over the last 70 years forces the question then – where did it all go wrong? Amidst the quiet gloating and condescending sense of satisfaction felt by many, one can understand why this question is acutely rehearsed, yet such a view of Britain is fraught with myopia. Too many historians and intellectuals link the interrogation of Englishness with the demise of its empire. England's identity is not bound by its territories. Englishness was structured and grounded long before her commonwealth formed and has solidly existed for over a thousand years. England shall continue to affirm itself long after the last remnants of the empire fade. Writers from this empire, in using the tools of postcolonial historiography, indulge in attributing England with a broken history of cultural hegemony and her territorial integrity now in tatters from the tide of multiculturalism. This consensus is insipidly dependant on the belief in the centrality of empire to the constitution of the English identity. Postcolonial views are often constricted temporally. The English question goes much deeper than the last two hundred years.

Readers may have already noticed the interchangeable lexicons of England and Britain. Britain of course is used when referring to any period after 1707 (the year the United Kingdom was forged, although the idea of a United Britain went as far back as the Saxons) in recognition of the deeply respected contributions of Wales and Scotland to England's imperial ambitions of expansion. It would be fair to say that 'being British' has been more about a shared sense of citizenship, whereas being English, Scottish, Irish or Welsh embedded a powerful emotional connotation. Being British in this sense carries no relation to ethnicity with a fascinating demarcation between the Anglo-Saxons and their Celtic neighbours. In the British context, English nationalism has largely been ignored or supressed, with England being at the centre of power, authorities deemed it wise never to encourage it. This has allowed in recent years for Scotland, Wales and Ireland to consistently reassert their own national sentiments over an apparent muted English voice. The Union has heavily relied on the relationship between England and Scotland. With a rich history of fighting between the two nations, English armies of the past have been generally more successful on the battlefield but Scotland has never really been subjugated. The formation of Britain enforced politics of mutual respect, restrain and complicity between the two peoples, but despite England having always dominated the Union, the Celtic tribes have never been forced to become English. The concept of the United Kingdom has never provided a viable alternate identity for its inhabitants, but what divides the home nations has always been less important than what unites them when confronting the rest of the world. A closer look at the early bloodlines of Britain is explored in the following chapter. The final chapter shall consider the implications for the English identity in light of the pending Scottish referendum on independence and the eternal debate over Britain's relationship with Europe.

The next chapter takes a closer look at the early formation of England and the very foundations of England's existence. Subsequent chapters go on to look in detail at the great war leaders that have had a significant impact and lasting influence on English culture and heritage. It is important to note that due to the compact nature of this book, it is impossible to justify or reflect in any great detail on all the eventualities of the lives of these extraordinary men. What has been included is perhaps their most valuable and memorable contributions and glories which still resonate with us today. England as a distinguished state, somehow managed to grow, survive and radiate waves of influence across the world over a relatively very long time. It recovered from modernity's inaugural revolution during the seventeenth century and continued to concentrate its power, defend its territories and developed a merciless capacity for violence. Whether such imperial aggression truly reflects the common nature of English people remains to be explored further. Such a study of national character might arguably be better conducted by someone who is objectively not English, the problem being, as George Orwell pointed out, outsiders rarely understand what Englishness is. It's often the little things. Churchill once said 'They [the British] are the only people who like to be told how bad things are-who like to be told the worst'. It's true, we do relish in disappointing news, and furthermore, we love a good moan about it. A civilisation of respectable queuing, weekend binge-drinking, the football, 'the back garden, the fireside, and the nice cup of tea', eighteenth century cottages, Remembrance Sunday, native peoples, southern charm, northern grit, land of hope and glory, rule Britannia...whilst always maintaining 'a deep moral attitude' and 'privateness' towards life. Such predictable and cliché concepts barely scratch the surface.

Despite the many identity crossroads in Britain; North and South, Cockney as opposed to the Geordie, working class, middle class, Scots, Welsh, Scouser, Yorkshire man etc., the nation, at the sight of 'an enemy' manages 'to close ranks'(or has done so at least until now). Multiple identities are frequently in play at any one time. England is constantly up for debate, more so now due to a steady revival of interest in history after a lengthy period of very low enthusiasm for the subject. Such a revival is perhaps ignited by the urgent necessity to reassess who we are. To do so, one must surely look back to see how we got here, to decipher the relevant chapters of history. All nations rise and fall. They perform well or they perform badly, they become well managed or mismanaged. In England, previous generations had the luxury of being brought up with the identity-affirming ideology of British Imperialism, owning a huge empire, and the British state at the centre, a state beyond question. The youth of today have no such luxury, feeling the ephemerality of invincibility and paying the price of previous prestige and glamour with an inevitable vacuum of national direction (and wealth). By the end of the 90's, there was a realisation that Britain wasn't what it once was. Over a decade into the twenty first century and Britain seems to have forgotten completely its personal history. Apathy reinforces a sense that we have now crossed a fundamental line; our final chapter has opened and waiting to be written.

E.M. Forster, while writing a critical barrage on England's middle class and their traditional attachment to 'the public-school' sphere (a background he himself came from), in his own liberal and humanistic way, unveils a less Anglocentric view by claiming the English:

> ...Go forth into a world that is not entirely composed of public school-men or even Anglo-Saxons, but of men who are as various as the sands of the sea; into a world of whose richness and subtlety they have no conception. They go forth into it with well-developed bodies, fairly developed minds, and underdeveloped hearts. And it is this underdeveloped heart that is largely responsible for the difficulties of Englishmen abroad...

Ignoring the blatant Marxist type critique on the middle classes, maybe Forster picks up on an important trait about the English character involving matters of the 'heart'. Expressing 'great joy or great sorrow' always takes a back seat compared to a more composed and dignified manner. Only on 'special occasions' are our true emotions allowed to surface. Regardless of the large disparity of wealth between the classes in England (which has always been there), there are quantum mechanical threads which seem to connect the nation together phenomenally creating occasional moments when the whole collective face the same direction. Orwell described it like a 'herd of cattle facing a wolf'. Though the English are not talented at expressing emotions, patriotism is an avenue which offers compensation. Like all nations, the working class is profoundly more insular and xenophobic in outlook, with far less toleration of all things foreign. Paradoxically, juxtaposing their insularity is the way they expose themselves with astonishing openness to the different cultures of the world.

When considering Englishness, humour as a social tool cannot be ignored. The British utilise irony on a daily basis, irony which is deeply entrenched in every day humour. British jokes tend to include dark or sarcastic undercurrents and are more subtle than their continental counterparts. There is more often than not a hidden meaning. It is possible that this type of humour originates from the perception that British culture is more conservatively reserved. Studies suggest that we use more humour overall than other nations, and comparatively have a reputation for being consistently funnier. Throughout history the use of humour in social interactions is, and has been, a very important convention in England. Bill Bryson noted: 'Watch any two Britons and see how long it is before they smile or laugh over some joke or pleasantry. It won't be more than a few seconds'. As our appetite for humour has developed, we have expanded several types of humour, considerably most of it employing linguistic creativity which gravitates around social norms. As we constantly attempt to find humour in the majority of circumstances we find ourselves, such hilarity among the English tends to manifest itself predominantly in times of personal hardship. The repudiation of taking one's own death seriously is undoubtedly a common English trait often perplexing to other nationalities. Such a mentality has had its merits in dreary times of conflict. George Mikes held that 'The English are the only people in the world who enjoy dying'. Though a little dramatic, this statement testifies to a darkness surrounding English humour, a gloominess which cheerfully trivialises the finality of death. Generally, the English philosophical position, ontologically, suspects that there is no all-encompassing meaning to life, thus instead of being intimidated by such beliefs, there is a tendency to twist it around to a vantage point of comedy. This is dia-metrically opposed to Europeans who traditionally find the theme of one's own death most uncomfortable. Existentialism as a school of thought never did quite take off in England like it did in Europe. The kind of fixed beliefs in existentialism seem to have a depressing effect on us. One of humour's most significant functions in England is to soften the psychological and emotional effects of misfortune. It is a prevailing antidote to hopelessness when all else seems lost. Humour is an undiminishing element within the English identity which still thrives throughout modern generations. The English have always prided themselves on their ability of self-mockery coupled with sarcasm directed at foreigners who take themselves too seriously. It has become a form of affection for each other based on a 'permitted self-veneration without vanity' and 'pride through parodic pantomime'.

This use of language and the role of language philosophy are crucial in sustaining the concept of Englishness. Philosophers Hume, Lock and Berkeley are often credited with the English tradition of empiricism, explicitly advocating the rejection of metaphysical speculation and theoretical abstract ideas and championing experience-led common sense as the method of understanding. This is in contrast to the traditional European philosophical trend of rationalism based on innate wisdom. Empiricism inclines towards a type of pragmatic methodology which considers itself to be a form of enlightened scepticism towards the great French and German philosophers, whose rationalism indulges in metaphysical ideology. This philosophical divide between Britain and Europe is in itself an interesting note. It remains clearly evident that the British are pulled by their empirical nature, unconsciously rendering theory and logic as a mere afterthought in the shadow of valourising experience and emotions. In light of England's recent negative experiences (the deconstruction of her empire and hugely mismanaged waves of immigration), its philosophical tendencies are perhaps contributing to its increasingly problematic identity. A percentage of the population feel, in a politicised fashion, that exalting England as a fledging multicultural society has served primarily to denounce Englishness as a myth or illusion reducing it to a social construct leniently giving way to a focus on plural ethnicity and multiculturalism. Enoch Powell's highly controversial rhetoric during the 1960's echoed the fact that Britain is an island which always has and always will embrace different cultures but not at the expense and erosion of the indigenous culture. Arguably using racist language or the preamble of national dogmatism; it is interesting to note that his words had considerable support across the population at the time. A time where Britain pragmatically, but reluctantly joined the European Community in 1973.

Following on from the ideas mentioned, the concept of Englishness could be conceived as a shining example of what Baudrillard termed a 'simulacrum'. That is to say, the *ideal* notion of Englishness is potently more real than what is expressed in carnal reality. It is not unreal but hyper-real. The Englishness that exists and manifests corporally cannot be adequately exchanged for what it's attempting to simulate. In other words, the Englishness of our imagination is unobtainable yet lies in the hyper-real of our consciousness – the imitation or replication of Englishness never really accomplishes what it's attempting to simulate. It also appears much easier to perform Englishness than it is to arduously define it. In trying to understand Englishness, one must be flexible and constantly oscillate between the gentleman and the larger lout, quiet conservatism and ostentatious patriotism, humility and superiority, rurality and urbanity, centre and periphery, pre-colonial and postcolonial. What can be mistaken for a highly unstable identity, Englishness instead should be attributed with a large degree of elasticity.

There is strong evidence to suggest that the Protestant Reformation during the seventeenth century had a profound impact on the national ethos of England, a country which became suspicious and wary of foreign influences particularly catholic states such as Spain, France, Italy and Germany with their infectious cultures of ornamentation and artificiality - diametrically opposing Protestantism's ideology of plainness. This factor is scrutinised more closely in chapter 4 with the legend of Oliver Cromwell – iconic of protestant austerity. The wealth from trade in the following centuries enabled

England to raise armies against these nations with considerable ease. Armies such as Marlborough's against Louis XIV, the armies of the electors of Hanover in Germany (interestingly now our current monarchs), Nelson's victorious fleet against the Spanish Armada and Wellington's army against Napoleon in the early nineteenth century and the list goes on. Certainly, at least in ideological terms, the English identity began to rapidly detach itself from catholic Europe during the seventeenth century and has continued to do so ever since. Oscar Wilde indeed turned to Catholicism as a means of rejecting the ethos of Victorian England and the values of the English establishment. His own problematic identity and tendency to reinvent himself originated from his obsession with France and his Irish roots – Irishness at the time being considered non-existent and France the 'old enemy'. Quite often a juxtaposing identity is needed; on these grounds then identity can be defined as a cultural negotiation formed from one of personal affections and desires. Binary identities are frequently understated. Chapter 3 looks closely at how England and France were (and sometimes still are) throughout history locked in such a relationship – a context of cultural affirmation by contrast to the other.

The geography of Britain cannot be overlooked as an element affecting its self-perception. Britain as a concept is easy to grasp – it is an island, surrounded by sea, distinguished from the mainland. Looking out across the water often invokes an insular sensation, a feeling of difference, a measure of belonging to a completely different culture; an alienating process which encourages a sense of detachment. Being an Island people, we expect to share more differences than similarities, as Shakespeare eloquently termed 'This happy breed of men, this little world, this precious stone, set in the silver sea', consistently reinforces our psychology of separation from Europe. There is always strong imagery association between Englishness and its countryside. The English countryside as an idyllic, quaint, peaceful, beautiful, picturesque and a distinct place free from the conflicting relations of race and class was exacerbated by industrialisation and its fragmentation of social communities and urbanisation. Rural studies have shown in reality, however, that rural racism does exist with visible minorities often perceived to be challenging the dominant definition of rurality. Iconic landmarks also embody Englishness – the White Cliffs of Dover being one of the most recognised features of England, emerging after the Second World War as a symbol of 'home' synonymous with 'victory'.

National characters have been used to represent the English identity. One such character is the eighteenth century John Bull, a heroic archetype of the Anglo-Saxon country Englishman, often depicted in a top hat and waist coat bearing the colours of Britain. The image of a stocky, well humoured conservative, a country squire who likes a beer, was regularly contrasted with a scrawny feeble wine-supping French revolutionist. His surname equated him with 'virile, strong and stubborn' traits; the French in response created the nick-name 'les rosbifs' (the roast beefs) for the English. Washington Irving described him as

> Plain, downright, matter-of-fact fellow, with much less of poetry about him than rich prose.

There is little of romance in his nature, but a vast deal of a strong natural feeling. He excels in humour more than in wit; is jolly rather than gay; melancholy rather than morose; can easily be moved to a sudden tear or surprised into a broad laugh; but he loathes sentiment and has no turn for light pleasantry. He is a boon companion, if you allow him to have his humour and to talk about himself; and he will stand by a friend in a quarrel with life and purse, however soundly he may be cudgeled.

Contemporary politicians have gone out of their way to avoid the issue of Englishness, through fear of undermining the United Kingdom as a whole; they have preferred altogether to advocate the strengthening of Britishness. No such restraints have been imposed on Scottishness or Welshness which have been allowed to flourish. From 1997, Tony Blair and Gordon Brown were amongst the most vocal campaigners of Britishness and vigorously defended the multinational, multi-ethnic vision of Great Britain. Since then, there have been numerous attempts from various intellectuals and politicians to put forward a less restricted visualisation of Englishness, one that is not purposefully subdued and inhibited. It is perhaps at this juncture where liberal/left politicians feel uneasy about the celebration or promotion of Englishness. If we regard Englishness as a cultural identity in its own right, then no matter how reluctantly, we have to concede two points. One, it cannot in itself be 'multicultural'. We can assume presently that England is a multicultural centre, or conceive that Britain is a multicultural state, but we cannot say that Englishness itself is multicultural, because a *culture*, by its very definition, cannot be. If so, it can no longer be classified as a culture and becomes something else. Secondly, English identity must be by its nature exclusive, basically because all identities are. An Aristotelian principle; something cannot be and not be at the same time. If you identify yourself as one thing you cannot be something else, however all-encompassing that something is. Modern debates have continuously tried to evade this by employing the discourse of 'multiple identity theories' when analysing the individual; an interesting approach but opens up a kind of infinite regress and will only take us so far.

Englishness, like any other cultural identity, must necessarily be defined by what it isn't as much as what it is. It remains difficult to dispute that people in Scotland and Wales feel more Scottish and Welsh now than they did twenty years ago. That is perhaps not a bad thing. Diversity is to be celebrated. But what about England? Encouraged by our reluctance to define ourselves, the English are still struggling to distinguish themselves from being British. There is no question that the BNP are a racist party, however, they will continue to rally support from the disenfranchised sections of England who are no longer buying into the 'multicultural and political correctness' of which they've been force-fed; a good example being 'National Diversity Day' now having more emphasis than St George's Day. Englishness should be a binding identity that welcomes all who embrace its values. There must be a nucleus to bind to. There must be a civilisational framework. Identities have varying gradations of elasticity, it appears that they get 'construed, constructed, misconstrued and deconstructed' but amidst the malaise there always remain fixed properties. The time may be approaching for England to reassert herself. Fashion fluctuates, tastes change, not many would identify with T.S.Eliot's England consisting of 'cup finals, the dog races, the pin table, the dart board, Wensleydale cheese, boiled cabbage cut in sections, beetroot in vinegar, 19th-century gothic churches…'and as Orwell identified as being 'bound up with solid breakfasts and gloomy Sundays, smoky towns and winding roads, green fields and red pillar-boxes'. Despite constant hegemonic federalisation from the juddering European Union and many traditional ways of seeing England in free fall, there has been an English identity since at least 900AD and we have continued to call our land England ever since.

The point about St George's Day being the most under-celebrated day throughout the United Kingdom is an interesting issue to probe, and lies at the very heart of this enquiry. France has Bastille Day, America has 4th July, both on par with the celebratory magnitude of St Patrick's and St David's Day and all are bank holidays in their respective countries. So why oh why is St George's day so subdued? There is perhaps an unfortunate anxiety about waving the English flag through fear of being categorised as a member of the EDL or associated with football hooliganism. There is some truth in that the flag has been tarnished with far right groups in the past. There are, however, deeper identity issues at play which are rooted firmly in history. St Patrick's, St Andrew's and St David's Day all share a common denominator which is based on an identity asserting itself against a dominant culture. The Irish, Scottish and Welsh days of celebration are intensified through a sense of retaliation from centuries of feeling devalued and oppressed – this has been exacerbated in recent years with the devolution process of the home countries. These national days are an opportunity to affirm 'cultural distinctness'. English people do not seem to share these needs of asserting their cultural heritage in the same way, yet there are signs of this changing. Discourses of devolution and independence in Ireland, Scotland and Wales have reestablished an affinity with their historic cultural identities whereas England has never lost its sense of sovereignty. Passive to others, as long they do not interfere with English lives and values, the English look on and go about their daily lives. Perhaps the English do not have the same urge to define themselves. Maybe locality comes first, for instance Londoners are very territorial and the north/south divide in England is very significant in the way we perceive each other. The youth of England have a right to celebrate their identity as much as the next country and should never be discouraged from waving the red cross. England grows quietly discontent at the muting of its voice. The political classes neglecting England in this way are making a catastrophic mistake.

It must be noted that France, a very real and dangerous threat to Britain during the eighteenth and nineteenth centuries, contributed significantly to British nationalism. During these centuries, a succession of wars broke out including 1689-1697, 1702-1713, 1743-1748, 1756-1763, 1778-1783, 1793-1802 and finally between 1803 and the concluding battle of Waterloo in 1815. All of these wars were fought fiercely with genuine hatred and multilayered rivalry, even during the peace times both sides plotted and schemed the other's demise. This prolonged struggle altered the dynamics of state power on both sides. For Britain it resulted in the foundation of the Bank of England and the creation of a titanic military machine which has been in steady decline since the end of the Second World War. During the eighteenth and nineteenth centuries, the British, unlike their European neighbours, had the luxury of celebrating many military victories and boasted the only European nation not to have succumbed to an invasion of an enemy force. The wars with France played a vital role in defining Great Britain; these wars between 1689 and 1815 (often called the second hundred years war) were religious, political and economic in nature. After 1778, France sided with America and smugly facilitated America's independence, the most valuable and much loved territory of Britain. The Napoleonic Wars presented a greater threat of invasion on home soil. Chapter 3 takes a closer look at this long and entertaining rivalry between England and France going back to the Hundred Years War, where Henry V began to forge a united Englishness defined collectively against the French 'other'. Britain (centuries later) in many ways came together through confrontation with European outsiders, not through the union of cultures, but united in reaction against a common enemy from across the channel. Great Britain was forged by war, not a cultural consensus. Here resides a very contemporary issue concerning the United Kingdom. The fact that Europeans have ceased fighting each other seems to leave Britain with no more adhesive to keep it together. Alex Salmond is already pushing for Scottish independence with considerable support, the Scottish referendum looming around the autumn of 2014. The construction of Britain was not on the whole successful in symphonically merging the Welsh, Scottish and English identities. Protestantism (as opposed to European Catholicism) was one of its binding properties but this is now only a residual element, a fading essence of its culture. In fact, now Britain is a part of the European Union, it remains very difficult to define itself against Europe at all. Politicians over the last fifteen years or so have heavy-handedly given sovereignty in particular areas of governance to Brussels, no matter how agonising this is for some Britons. The re-emergence of Welsh, Scottish and English patriotism is currently responding and flourishing under the wider loss of a British identity. It is distinctly possible that Britishness may not survive. An inconceivable thought seventy years ago. In contrast to a union built on conciliatory sentiments, Britain's merging of nations underpinned by outward aggression is evident in the popular song first composed by James Thomson in 1740:

When Britain first, at Heaven's command

Arose from out the azure main;
This was the charter of the land,
And guardian angels sang this strain:
"Rule, Britannia! rule the waves:
"Britons never will be slaves."
The nations, not so blest as thee,
Must, in their turns, to tyrants fall;
While thou shalt flourish great and free,
The dread and envy of them all.
"Rule, Britannia! rule the waves:
"Britons never will be slaves."
Still more majestic shalt thou rise,

More dreadful, from each foreign stroke;
As the loud blast that tears the skies,
Serves but to root thy native oak.
"Rule, Britannia! rule the waves:
"Britons never will be slaves."

This song in many ways symbolises the heart of the Union; notice much more emphasis is placed on overseas conquest, 'ruling the waves', defeating 'foreign' 'tyrants' etc. Britain was not assembled out of a desired unity or oneness, but out of a defensive necessity to survive and constant threats from Europe.

Anglo-French relations slowly improved until 1963, when, after all Britain had done for France during the Second World War, General de Gaulle rejected Britain's first application to join the EEC. This reignited vigorous anti French feelings in England which were not as intensely reciprocated in France. From that point on, General de Gaulle lost any respect from Britain and as well as becoming a figure of our Francophobic indulgence, he came to represent the French as untrustworthy allies. Churchill. In 1940, magnanimously offered France mutual citizenship as Germany was occupying everything north of the river Loir. This offer was rejected outright. This train of thought leads us once again to perhaps the most important question of our era. If Britain survives, what is its true relationship with Europe? As integral as it is to the pursuit of the English identity, the final chapter is reserved for this debate in more detail. The British public often remark that they are not educated enough to make an informed decision in answering this coveted question. The final chapter will look at the negatives and positives of Britain becoming further integrated with Europe considering cultural, financial and political factors. The final chapter will hopefully analyse what Britain actually gains and what it loses, or perhaps more precisely what it has lost measured by what it stands to gain. Before that though, this book is 'in search of the Lionheart Nation', trying to establish the foundations of England and reaffirming the rooted truth of our English identity. To do this adequately, one must surely go back to the beginning of our gene pool, to the founders of England. It will not suffice to simply consider the last few hundred years. This period will tell us much about the formation of Britain and the British Empire but not enlighten us too much on England. It is the genetic origins of England and the construction and maintenance of Englishness with which this work is historically concerned with. England's sense of self-superiority or what is often construed as an egotistical form of national arrogance, does not just originate from past military victories. England has an extensive portfolio consisting of 44% of all the world's inventions (particularly during the Industrial Revolution), including the first internal combustion engine, splitting the atom, the world wide web, the jet engine, calculus, televisions, underground networks, telephones, electricity, DNA fingerprinting, microchips, cell biology, electromagnetic induction and radar to mention just a tiny selection. Great men such as Francis Bacon, Isambard Kingdom Brunel, Isaac Newton, John Cockcroft and Michael Faraday led the way and set England above the rest. Frantz Fanon once stated 'The claim to a national culture in the past...rehabilitates that nation and serves as a justification for the hope of a future national culture'. That is also this books' intention.

CHAPTER 2

England's Roots – Tracing the Genealogy of Englishness

From approximately 400AD, with the complete with-drawal of the Roman Empire from the British Isles, Europe plunged into what is commonly known as the Dark Ages. This period, although stretching all the way to the tenth century, is termed 'Dark' precisely because our knowledge of this era is patchy at best. Only a few comprehensive written sources exist which originated throughout these crucial six hundred years, the most significant (in tracing English identity) being the *Anglo-Saxon Chronicles*. There are other sources such as the work produced by the monk Venerable Bede, in the 8th century. He provided an insight into the life of Saxon-Viking England in his *Historia Ecclesiastica Gentis Anglorum*. Other written sources such as *Historia Brittonum* and the *Annales Cambriae* are quite fascinating yet fraught with folklore myths and legends and should be viewed with an open and interpretive mind. Unfortunately, many of the dates used in this chapter are to be treated with trepidation as when com-paratively contrasting modern historical documents, one comes across many contradictions concerning temporal accuracy. It is the dark ages after all. Thankfully we have numerous archeological remnants of the dark ages in Britain such as Hadrian's Wall and the discovery of Viking hoards at Sutton Hoo in East Anglia. It is during this murky past that the early ideas of Englishness began to stir.

For Rome, the Northern provinces such as England were merely outposts garrisoned to help protect Roman territories from the constant menace of barbarian attacks. Evidence suggests that the Romans never migrated to Britain in large numbers, and those that did, besides military personnel, mostly left when Rome realised it could no longer defend its northern conquests. England was particularly difficult to protect as from 400AD it was attacked by the Picts from the North (the reason for building Hadrian's Wall), contended with Celtic aggression from Ireland and Wales and an enormous pending incursion from the Angles and Saxons from North Germany. When the Anglo-Saxons attacked England in 408 there were hardly any Roman forces left to defend it. Rome perhaps felt at some point, in letting Britain fall into the hands of the Germanic peoples, it could someday return and retake the Isles. Little did Rome know that it would never have Britain on its agenda again. It is this rapidly evolving period that historians know shockingly little, particularly of what was happening north of the English Channel.

What we do know is that the incoming peoples of the fifth and sixth centuries, mostly consisting of Angles and Saxons from north-west Germany, with a few Jutes from Denmark and Frisians from the Low Countries, immigrated to England in much larger numbers than their Roman predecessors. The lexicon 'Saxon' was often used by the Romans to refer to all the German tribes. Germania was not a coherent nation in the modern sense but was divided into three main tribes – Saxons, Franks and Bavarians. These were the most well-known tribes to the writers of imperial Rome, who noted that each tribe had their own laws, customs and historic traditions. According to Roman transcripts, the Saxons remained heathen the longest, were the fiercest warriors and were the most difficult to Romanise out of all the Germanic tribes. They were also hereditary enemies of the Franks, who later moved into Gaul and modern day France. In contrast, the Bavarians were the softest of the tribes and became heavily Romanised. So the Franks moved into Gaul laying the foundations of Charlemagne's future great empire and the Anglo-Saxons took England amidst the vacuum left by Rome. Much later in 800AD, the Frankish chieftain, Charlemagne, forged a large empire across Europe - a turning point noted by historians as the final shift in power from southern Europe to Northern Europe. Romans had a reputation for betraying the trust of loyal barbarian tribes for their own imperial gains. The barbarian peoples did not understand and hated the imperial civilisation that was imposed on them, and all except the Franks and Anglo-Saxons adopted Christianity before crossing the imperial frontiers.

Reasons why the Anglo-Saxons decided to leave Saxony remains open to speculation. Some historians have suggested that the land level in the coastal areas of north Germania was sinking in the fifth and sixth centuries causing severe flooding, thus the inhabitants reacted by making the crossing to Britain. It is noted that in 400 the Rhine was constantly patrolled by the Romans and marked a clear dividing line between Roman civilisation and barbarian wilderness. Perhaps through constant Roman annoyance they decided to leave? There could have been multiple reasons which we can only really second guess. As the Romans left Gaul and the Franks moved in, they came to enjoy what the Romans had established - largely a healthy taxation system and a sound infrastructure. This made the Franks the wealthiest tribe in all Europe. The Anglo-Saxons, however, kept very little of what was once Roman.

Something the Anglo-Saxons and the Celts had in common was there dislike for anything Roman including the cities that the Romans built. Traditionally, Saxon leaders lived in great halls and the common people in wooden or mud huts. Ironically the Celts and Britons must have looked upon the Anglo-Saxon incursion as the Saxons perceived the later Viking invasions. Excavations at the Bernician palace in Northumberland suggest the Angles took over a pre-existing political centre where Anglian chieftains would have initially ruled over a majority of early Britons. Further south, however, majority of the Anglo-Saxon settlement took place, destroying towns, structures and even the newly established religion of Christianity brought by the Romans quickly disappeared. Descendants of the Roman civilians retreated to various kingdoms such as Cornwall, north of the border and Wales. The word 'Welsh' was the Saxon term for 'foreigner' and was used to describe non-Saxons but the Celtic speaking people avidly fought for independence in these kingdoms and the Anglo-Saxons largely left them alone. This interestingly mirrors the modern day relationship England has with the rest of the United Kingdom.

We know from Venerable Bede in his writings *Historia Ecclesiastica Gentis Anglorum* – *Ecclesiastical History of England* that the Anglo-Saxons gradually became Christian which was facilitated by the missionary St Augustine who was dispatched from Rome. As the nature of Anglo-Saxon life was largely tribal, there had been no overall king of the country who adopted Christianity and consequently no tradition of unity. Anglo-Saxons simply recognised their kind as different from Celts or Romans. The man at the helm of each group of barbarians in Saxon civilisation was called the 'cyning' ('man from the kin') in Old English. The Saxons had a tradition of only electing an overall king ('rex' in Latin) in a time of great threat or emergency. Bede tells us that the Saxons did not have a king but were ruled by 'satraps' or tribal chiefs and only when the whole people were threatened did they elect a war leader. The Frankish and Anglo-Saxon rulers were primarily war leaders in contrast to their Celtic and continental equivalents. Somewhere between 410 and 900, England was divided into several Anglo-Saxon kingdoms, the main ones being East Anglia, Mercia, Northumbria, Wessex, Sussex and Kent. It is worthy to note, in the backdrop to St Augustine's arrival to an emerging England, all the Germanic peoples except the Franks and the Anglo-Saxons were Arian Christians. In fact the Western Church had never been Arian. The important difference being that the Arian conception of Jesus Christ is that the Son of God did not always exist and is thus not eternal, but was created by God the Father generating a fundamental distinction. This conviction is embedded in the Gospel of John 14:28 where it states "You heard me say, 'I am going away and I am coming back to you.' If you loved me, you would be glad that I am going to the Father, for the Father is greater than I". Arianism is said to originate from the teachings of Arius which are in opposition to conventional Trinitarian Christianity where emphasis lies in the Holy Trinity where the Nicene (Catholic) position stress the verse "I and the Father are one" (John 10:30). At the time the heathen barbarians with their pagan beliefs were seen as just simple-minded as opposed to the far more deviant and dangerous Arian Christians. Ironically, the two peoples who were largely responsible for the rise of the Papacy in later years were indeed the Franks and Anglo-Saxons, and the Anglo-Saxons were the only group to have preserved classical learning during the eighth century.

Before Augustine arrived, the process of Anglo-Saxon migration to England broke up many tribal groupings and brought new war leaders to the surface. Such leaders attained loyalty and power by gathering warriors around them who were compensated with the spoils of war such as gold, precious objects and land. The Saxons were the first to bring this militarised type of community to the growing identity of England, where warriors had a new status in society. This is strongly reflected in contemporary Anglo-Saxon literature too, with the emergence of the great heroic poetry of *Beowulf* emanating from the period; a tale set in Scandinavia about a heroic fearless Norse warrior aiding terrorised towns with his band of Geats and Thanes. Such legends were evidently prevalent on Anglo-Saxon minds and were significant influences on the collective conscience, compounded further perhaps by the Viking raids later. This culture of heroic warriorism no doubt had its roots in many pagan traditions later mixed with Norse mythological beliefs, for example; Odin and the final battle at Ragnorok where all the fallen warriors will be gathered for the final fight. The greatest warriors would be hand-picked by Odin straight from the battlefield, collected by the Valkyries and taken to the Halls of Valhalla where they ate and drank at Odin's table. To die fighting was the best, most honorable way to die. Interestingly, the idea of the dying warrior being collected by Valkyries is remarkably similar to the modern incantations of the folksong 'Swing Low Sweet Chariot' adopted by the English, giving the image of angel-type figures carrying off the fallen to a place of merriment beyond this world. This also explains how at many Anglo-Saxon burials, lavish weapons, long swords with golden-jeweled pommels and coinage have been found to have laid with the man in his grave. St Augustine helped change these archaic beliefs, as by the time the Vikings got here, the Anglo-Saxons viewed their Scandinavian cousins as pagans, heathens and entirely unchristian.

Augustine troubled himself with trying to answer the question as to why the Roman Empire had fallen, most notably in his great work *De Civitate Dei* or *City of God* consisting of twenty-two books written over thirteen years between 413 and 426. The barbarians were convinced that the Roman Empire had fallen because it had deserted Christianity and chose the pagan gods. St Augustine knew the pagan beliefs well and only converted to Christianity himself at the age of thirty-two. He made it his mission to explain to the barbarians why the Christian God had allowed the Roman Empire to fall and the greatness of Rome to be sacked. His convincing message was that God, being omnipotent and ordaining all that happens in heaven and earth, almighty and righteous, rightfully willed the destruction of Rome as it had not ruled justly. The fact that he himself was so distraught at Rome's demise revealed to him how little he understood the will of God. Men in general were perhaps incapable of seeing why Rome fell because eternity cannot be seen by mortal men and women. His point to the barbarians was that the fall of Rome did not matter as nothing earthly is supremely good in itself, and that justice was more important than the state. This had a profound impact on the Anglo-Saxon kingdoms and by the time of Alfred the Great in 849, Christianity once more graced the British Isles. It seems quite likely that due to the geographical position of England and its ethnic and cultural similarities, England would have eventually reached political unification of its sub-kingdoms, but the re-emergence of Christianity along with the Viking invasions helped accelerate England's granite bond.

The fifth to the eighth centuries confusingly culminates in extensive lists of King names and battles making it hard to focus with any clarity on developments during this hazy period. Some historians have estimated there may have been as many as two to three hundred different kings across northern Europe at this time. It seems more practical to perhaps look at one or two kings from different tribes to build up an accurate picture. One such leader was King Rædwald of the East Angles. Rædwald was baptised in Kent under the Overlord of King Æthelberht, however, due to Rædwald's pagan wife constantly manipulating him, Venerable Bede tells us that he practiced his religious faith at a pagan and Christian altar in the same place of worship. By 616 Rædwald managed to make his kingdom the strongest in southern England. We also know that he took his army north to the kingdom of Northumbria (once Bernicia and Deira now merged into one) and defeated his Anglian rival King Æthelfrith. The curious archaeological discovery at Sutton Hoo in 1938 has led many to speculate, with its enigmatic artefacts and golden objects, that it might be the tomb of King Rædwald. Some suspect it belonged to Alfred the Great himself but as no body accompanied the ship-burial it remains hard to tell. We know that King Rædwald did not venture north of Hadrian's Wall, although the majority of Lowland Scots were not Celtic in ethnicity but Anglo-Saxon or Norse. The inhabitants of Southern Scotland had more in common with the people of northern England than their Highland countrymen. The Highlanders called the inhabitants of southern Scotland and England 'Sassenach' which in Gaelic means 'Saxon', a term modern Scots still use in reference to the English. The Highland Picts, much more Celtic in origin, found their southern countrymen almost indistinguishable from Anglo-Saxon. To the West, the Welsh tribe, also more Celtic in origin would distinguish themselves as not being 'Saison' meaning Saxon in their own language. If the Sutton Hoo findings in Ipswich are indeed that of the Angle King Rædwald, it does shed light on the intimate connections the Anglo-Saxons had with Scandinavia. The tradition of ship-burial is a Norse one; specifically Swedish and the helmet and shield corroborate this link, suggesting our King Rædwald of East Anglia probably originated from the Scandinavian Wulfing's bloodline running through Sweden. This would also support the Norse impact on Anglo-Saxon literature at the time such as *Beowulf* and *The Poetic Edda* - heroic poetry of the age. The famous Icelandic writer Snorri Sturluson and his *Heimskringla* (History of the Norwegian Kings) and *The Prose Edda* were also to become inextricably linked to England.

A little later came the next and probably the most powerful Saxon king in Alfred the Great. Born in 849 into the ruling dynasty of Wessex, he was the fifth son of King Æthelwulf who took the West Saxons to the zenith of their power. During Alfred's time, England was ever closer to nationhood, now composed of just Northumbria, Mercia, East Anglia and Wessex. All other kingdoms were subdued and dominated by these more powerful realms. Medieval writers began to distinguish these early Germanic invaders from their Roman-Celtic cohabitants, creating the term *Angli Saxones*. Such medieval writers on the continent, in coining the unifying term *Angli Saxones*, meant the very beginning of an English Identity. Though not unified in the national sense yet, there was a growing consensus of separateness from Anglo-Saxons and all other tribes. England's kingdoms would oscillate between war and peace as power shifted back and forth. Alfred was just a child when the first Vikings landed in East Anglia and would end up fighting them most of his life. It was Wessex (the West Saxons) that led the movement of the unification of England, most significantly under Alfred. He went on a pilgrimage to Rome with his father as a young man, concreting his Christian beliefs and enriching his education. In 865 the first 'Great

Army' of Vikings from Scandinavia, consisting of mostly Danes and Norwegians, arrived at East Anglia's coast and by the end of 870 had arrived on Alfred's frontier in Reading. A number of battles and skirmishes ensued with both Danes and Saxons claiming victories. It was here where Alfred's last remaining brother, Ethelred, was slain and Alfred took control of the kingdom.

Alfred found himself paying the Vikings silver in order to pacify the growing number of Scandinavians crossing the channel. The Anglo-Saxon Chronicles inform us that during Alfred's reign, he encouraged his people to read and write and that Alfred was promoting himself as leader of all the English kingdoms against the Vikings. It was during his dynasty that the Anglo-Saxon Chronicles were published. With the Angles in East Anglia, Mercia and Northumbria not able to withstand the tide of Norsemen led by Halfdan (leader of the Danes) Guthrum and Anund (other Viking leaders), it was not long before the Great Army turned its sights to Wessex. With a show of defiance, Alfred chased a large section of the army all the way to Exeter but failed to catch them in time before the Vikings entered their fortifications. This clearly intimidated the Vikings, leading them to hand over hostages and pledged oaths of allegiances to Alfred. As so often seems the case, this truce with the Vikings did not last long. By 875 they began to threaten and attack Wessex once again. The chronicles tell us that in 878 Alfred led an attack on Guthrum's Viking army where the Scandinavians were forced to make peace. They left Wessex to return to East Anglia, still having control of Northumbria, eastern Mercia and all of East Anglia. Alfred retained

Wessex and the West of Mercia. Consequently, Alfred and Guthrum drafted a treaty dividing the kingdom between them lasting for many years. The area controlled and occupied by the Danes came to be famously known as the Danelaw. Within this perimeter, all inhabitants both Saxon and Scandinavian subscribed to Danish Viking rule. This is potently evident in the nomenclature of place names spread throughout the region; good examples are place names with the suffix 'thorpe' such as Scunthorpe, Cleethorpes, Skelling-thorpe, Ugthorpe, Willsthorpe etc. The suffix 'thorpe' has Scandinavian and Germanic roots loosely meaning 'homestead'. Also place names ending in '*by*' such as Grimsby, Wetherby, Scremby, Digby being very similar to Danish place names such as Brondby and Lyngby. It is true that the region known as the Danelaw contained a unique mixture of Vikings and Anglo-Saxons and although the Danes clearly established their culture, they also adopted many ways of the English. South of the Danelaw, in the heart of Saxon territory, Alfred was said to have translated many Latin literary works himself. *The Anglo-Saxon Chronicles* has been viewed by some as acting as a Saxon propaganda tool against the Vikings. This inadvertently gives tribute to the Scandinavians, as without them the Anglo-Saxons would not have been able to unify under a solitary English banner.

This leads us to look at the Vikings themselves; after all, history suggests they are as responsible for developing Englishness as much as the Anglo-Saxons throughout England's infancy. So who exactly were the Vikings, why did they leave their place of origin and why are they actually called Vikings? The term 'Viking' has never really been investigated in any great detail. We know it was the name given to the Norsemen who descended on the British Isles from the wilderness of Scandinavia. Their fearsome reputation comes from their barbaric raids on the coastal monasteries, the first recorded Viking raid being at Lindisfarne in 793. Above all they were a warrior people who were attributed with great courage, great strength and had a reputation for being particularly bloodthirsty. They brought with them tales of their warriors who had slain trolls and other mythical creatures. Classic Viking heroes such as Egil and Grettir produced the concept of 'beserkers' – groups of Viking warriors who worked themselves up into a violent raging frenzy before going into battle. They are physically described as tall, broad shouldered, strongly built with often flowing blonde or red hair. Their life was generally hard and bleak. When they ceased fighting they were fishermen or farmers. They had no stone buildings and no such things as books or written documents; however, we know they adopted the Greek alphabet for their own various uses. A potential source for the word '*Viking*' could perhaps stem from the suffix '*wic*' which was given to a place where constant trading occurred. In East Anglia where they settled perhaps more than anywhere else in Europe, there are numerous places which show evidence of this Germanic linguistic pattern such as Norwich and Ipswich – notice the '*wich*' suffix which would have been pronounced '*wic*'. The word 'Viking' could have been a term for 'trader'. They had a reputation for trading all over the world and even traded with the Arab nations far away in the East. There is also the possibility that the name Viking came from the term 'Viken' referring to the area around the Oslo fjord. It is not difficult to imagine why the Vikings left their homeland when we look at the geography of Norway. The only land suitable for agriculture is sporadic patches by the coast; most of the country is mountainous and although beautiful and majestic it is not conducive for cultivating pastoral or arable farming. Also there is a chance that with a growing population they simply needed more space. Another theory is that many wished to escape the growing authority of their local Earls and Kings. Sweden though better terrain, has runestones referring to raids in England so the Swedes may have expanded for the same reason; although evidence points to them sailing mostly east into the Baltic states and the Rus (Russia).

Being phenomenal sailors, from 870 the Norwegians settled in Iceland and during the 900s reached parts of Greenland. We know they heavily settled on the Shetland and Orkney Islands where they found it relatively easy to move into Ireland and set up strongholds, founding the settlements of Cork and Dublin. Due to the mountainous fjords, vast forests and marshlands of Scandinavia, the most obvious way to travel for the Vikings would have been by water. With a culture so firmly based around water, it is no surprise that they were leaps above all others when it came to sailing. Their famous longboats had the most sophisticated design in all Europe and were simply better than their equivalents. *The Anglo-Saxon Chronicle* makes a significant reference to Norway by stating that the first ships arrived from somewhere called Hordaland; even today there is a province in southern Norway with the exact same name. One of the few documents relating to this region comes from a prolific traveller and writer named Ottar (or the

Anglo-Saxon interpretation 'Othere') who gives us a description of his homeland:

> The land of the Norwegians was very long and very narrow. All that they can graze or plough lies by the sea; and even that is very rocky in some places; and to the east, and alongside the cultivated land, lie wild mountains

Their mountains would have likely given them an abundant supply of Iron ore to make lavish weapons, many of which have been found around the various archaeological sites on the British Isles. This Norwegian writer gives us an insight into what the Vikings existing geographical knowledge was like, with ancient sea routes probably being passed down from generation to generation. As this Scandinavian writer frequented King Alfred's court, he told the Saxons how the land south of Norway was known as the region the Jutes and Angles inhabited and how the Finn tribe lived in the land to the North of Norway. With Ottar's writings and the Sutton Hoo discovery, there are growing subtle intimations that there was a far deeper and earlier Viking contact with the Anglo-Saxons, particularly in East Anglia.

So prevalent were the Viking invasions on the Orkney and Shetland Islands that Norse was the main language right up until the sixteenth century, until Gaelic took over. It still remains problematic to know the scale of immigration of Vikings to the British Isles. Linguists lean towards a large scale settlement suggesting numbers were quite high, but historians feel dubious about this assumption. The fact that there are hundreds of place names as well as family surnames which bear strong Viking connections would suggest a significant number was needed to have had such an impact. It could not have been just a few clans or tribes over several generations. Yet, their particular concentration on the extremities of the Isles suggests they did not fancy England's mainland, perhaps because of the immediate pending confrontation with the Saxons from the moment they disembarked their ships. During the Danelaw period, however, there existed a relative peace between England's new Viking settlers and the older Anglo-Saxon inhabitants. Some historians have suggested that the East Anglians and the Danish Vikings were more than happy to work and live together; the residents feeling threatened not by the incoming Vikings but by the West Saxons further south. What emerged in East Anglia particularly was an Anglo-Scandinavian hybrid culture, a merging of Scandinavian and Anglo-Saxon traditions. It was the hybridisation of these two cultures that led to the creation of a new identity. A primitive English identity; not Scandinavian or Saxon by recognition, but English.

The eleventh century saw England settle down somewhat but leading up to the famous battles of 1066, came new threats from overseas. England submitted to a Danish Chieftain, King Knut. By 1027 Knut had fused England, Denmark, Norway and part of Sweden into a Scandinavian empire. Knut died in 1035 and his empire was dismantled with his son and successor holding the English throne only until 1042, when the Anglo-Saxon monarchs re-ascended the throne with Edward the Confessor and Harold Godwinson. The new threats to England came from the Normans coming from the south, crossing the English Channel from Normandy and a new wave of Vikings led by Harald Hardrada (whose real name was Harald Sigurdsson) crossing the North Sea from Norway. Hardrada was a legendary warrior who served in Constantinople as a Varangian Guard before becoming the absolute ruler of Norway. The English (now consisting of Danes and Saxons fighting side by side), led by Harold Godwinson marched north to meet these final Viking invaders where the Battle of Stamford Bridge took place, lasting nearly all day. Despite the English having marched some two hundred miles from London, they defeated the Vikings and slayed Hardrada as the Norwegians broke ranks. It has been said that of the 330 ships that brought the Vikings across, only 24 were needed to carry the survivors back to Norway. The Battle of Stamford Bridge on 25 September 1066 marks the last Viking invasion of Britain, and, in a way, denotes the close of the Viking era. Such a heroic victory was marred by the news of the Norman arrival in the South, led by William of Normandy and later to be coined William the Conqueror. As the English waved goodbye to the Norsemen they found themselves begrudgingly greeting the Normans; marching quickly south, battle-tired and hungry, to give the Normans a traditional 'Welcome to England'.

At the Battle of Hastings in 1066, Harold's army miraculously almost defeated the Normans with William unable to break through the English shield wall. Only a foolish mistake to pursue the retreating Normans allowed the Saxons to be overrun by Norman superior cavalry. William of Normandy, through hereditary title now claimed the throne of England; but despite the majority of the aristocracy becoming Norman and speaking French, the masses in England remained English. The Normans did not immigrate on the scale of the Saxons or Vikings thus never really impacting on the existing gene pool. Norman-French never became the first language with the exception of the elite in the country. Any French that was spoken did not last long. But this was not William's intention. He did not want to convert England nor did he perceive his conquest as a colonial act, but of inheriting his land that belonged to him. He wished to preserve English as the national language, keeping documents in English and Latin. He reinvigorated the legal system but he did not replace it with a Norman one. Interestingly though, the Normans were not Scandinavian but had many Viking roots themselves as the Norsemen raided the north coast of France hundreds of years earlier, as well as England. This said, had it not have been for the Normans, England would have likely developed into a Scandinavian culture as opposed to a European culture and the English language would probably not have reached global linguistic hegemony. Old Norse, which was the language of the Vikings, and Old English were relatively similar linguistically, making it more than likely the Vikings and Anglo-Saxons could arguably understand each other. Both languages had more in common with present day German than modern English, but the fusion of Norse, Saxon and (to a lesser extent) the Latin-based French gave birth to the English language we use today.

This brief backdrop to England's development sets the scene and creates a fitting background to introduce our first Lionheart Leader who had his own significant impact on the English identity, Henry V. Perhaps England's most under-celebrated leader, the following chapter discusses the everlasting impact Henry V left on English culture and in the process marked the beginning of a real sense of unity and staged a turning point for the developing phenomenon of Englishness.

CHAPTER 3

Henry V:
Warrior King

Owre Kynge went fourth to Normandy,
With grace and might of chivalry;
The God for him wrought marvellously,
Wherefore Englonde may calle, and cry
...Then Forsooth that night comely
In Agincourt field he fought manly;
Through grace of God most mightily
He had both the field and the victory
Deo gratias Anglia redde pro victoria
The Agincourt Carol

The Hundred Years War was in many ways an extra-
ordinarily lengthy conflict by any parameters; a war
which has contributed so much to both England and
France's national identity that the feuds' lengthy period
echoes the lasting influence on national relations today.
Propagated by contrasting motives and contextualised
by European standards, it could effortlessly be depicted
as the war of all wars – giving rise to all the horrors
and spoils created and contested by two nations. During

this war, on 16 September 1386, a memorable king was born. This period is a very suitable starting point for the ontological study of nationalism in both countries, bound in adversity, filled with historical hatred and resentment; it gives birth to a primitive form of patriotism founding our national identities at present. From 1337 to 1453, France was the most advanced and wealthiest country in Europe and the recognized superpower of northern European culture; yet it was quite literally bullied, terrorized and held to ransom for over a hundred years by a kingdom across the channel - far smaller, less wealthy and with an inferior population. London at the time was by a long way the largest city of England with a population of around fifty thousand, the next largest cities being Bristol, Norwich and York bustling with about eight or nine thousand inhabitants. This was in contrast with Paris which boasted a population of over a hundred thousand.

War during this period was endemic and was virtually continuous along border regions such as northern England. This era was the zenith of chivalric knighthood and war was the occupation of knights – it was intrinsically a way of life. So much so, that when there was a rare absence of war, many became discontented and took up tournaments such as jousting, but this hardly replaced real combat. For the French, the ceaseless depredations of English invading armies uncannily parallel those of the marauding Scottish raids in the north of England. War was not always profitable but fighting could prove popular for many reasons. There is a significant number of chronicles expressing varying degrees of enthusiasm for obtaining glory in battle and the honors that accompany it; the romantic resonance of chivalry from Froissart's eulogies of the camaraderie and loyalty between knights in arms. As opposed to tales of great battle victories sung by the Bards and tales of heroism against unimaginable odds, the French lived it quite differently. For the people of France it was an abhorrent, horrifying and dreadful period which was experienced by entire communities and families. Undoubtedly, the Hundred Years War (with perhaps the exception of World War Two) contains Frances' darkest hour, as shall be scrutinized later with the Treaty of Troyes. While it is true that the atrocities committed in France unite historians in claiming England 'did France a great wrong', one has no doubt that had the roles been reversed (and they so nearly were on several occasions) France would have acted in exactly the same manner. Unconsciously this war has vigorously rooted itself concretely into national myth and has consequently affected Anglo-French relations ever since. It was in this tumultuous, gothic and rapidly developing world that England's hero king forged his legacy as the last of his kind.

Henry V is widely regarded, and rightly so, as the piece de resistance of English history embodying glory par excellence in military affairs as well as political and cultural leadership. Before a closer analysis of the man himself and his specific campaigns which extrapolate his notoriety, an account must be given of his lasting influence on the dawn of English patriotism. Up until Henry V, when evaluating overseas relations, it is a fair comment to say there was a form of national sentiment. Such feelings, however, were by no means dominant in the collective psyche of the period. A conscious awareness of national identity is a relatively complex notion and was rarely lived outside the educational elite. In fact, relations between knights on both French and English sides respectively were usually cordial and often felt closer to each other than ordinary soldiers on their own side. Nonetheless, in rudimental fashion, a man did draw distinction between himself and a member of another nation. An Englishman would more often think of himself as a Cornishman or Yorkshire-man before an Englishman, yet he had some idea of national identity by distinguishing Englishmen from foreigners. Mental attitudes, particularly of individuals remain difficult to ascertain, but an educated guess leads one to suspect that regionalism in England, before Henry V, entailed that a Londoner's attitude towards the Scots was very different than a Northumbrian. To one the Scot represented a constant menace and threat, but to the other just an inhabitant of some distant insignificant land. The Hundred Years War and specifically Henry V, for England, began to change this regionalist mentality.

A fourteenth century chronicler, Geoffrey Le Baker commentates on an incident which took place during a French raid on Southampton. The local militia had gained the upper hand through support from the surrounding area, and a French knight from the invading force was hacked to the ground by a young English peasant. The French knight requested quarter and offered to pay a large ransom 'Rançon', but the ruffian responded 'yes, I know you're a Francon', and proceeded to club him to death, not knowing the other's language. Le Baker narrates the story to reveal the differing attitudes to war between the knightly and non-knightly classes, but it also reveals how men perceived through different languages a clear conceived distinction between nations. People of the period employed two criteria to distinguish between nationalities – language and place of birth. Although Anglo-Norman was dying out, Henry insisted that all his correspondence was conducted in English. His father, Henry of Lancaster, unlike all the other monarchs before him, was coronated in English instead of Latin or French. Under Henry, English became the language of convocation. This went hand in hand with contemporary writers such as Wyatt, Chaucer, Malory and Langland who all principally wrote in English. England now possessed a common language within the kingdom. Only Cornish existed as a separate linguistic entity. The assertion of the English language as an aid in identifying nationhood shows an increasing measure of national self-awareness, reinforced by Henry's relentless insistence on religious practices, including the Bible, to be conducted in English. Such an atmosphere was preserved and consolidated a hundred and fifty years or so later, with Shakespeare, under Elizabeth I rule, who by enriching the language paid homage in writing the ever popular play 'Henry V'. This sense of growing nationalism under Henry V was, however, not the main reason for going to war with France.

Henry V is mostly famous for winning one battle – Agincourt. This remarkable triumph shall be evaluated in the pages to come, but Henry (whose real name was Harry) reflects far more facets of medieval history than the importance of merely winning battles. His pursuit of dynastic knight-errantry led him to spend most of his nine-year reign on foreign soil. Much awareness of our most coveted king emanates from Shakespeare. Ballad literature and poems like that of John Page on the siege of Rouen grew around him while he was alive, but after his untimely death the saga multiplied. Little is known of his childhood but we know much of his life was spent on the road, moving from one castle to another. To be present and commonly visible to one's subjects in different provinces had more than one advantage. He travelled with a large retinue, surrounding himself by writers, priests, strategists and nobility who followed him. At the age of fourteen, a typical squire, he learnt the skills for preparing for war with investiture as a knight. The retainers of the House of Lancaster who accompanied Henry were very well travelled and experienced in overseas campaigns. Some had fought as crusaders against the Turks or had pilgrimaged to the Holy Land – no doubt inspiring young Harry's future ambitions and dreams of future conquests.

It is on the road as a young man, that he would also have been told of the English claim to the crown of France and the chained glories of his ancestors' victories at Crecy and Poitiers. He was brought up on tales of chivalry – tales which convincingly made an impact on the man he was to grow into. Ideals held close to Henry were the virtues of skill at arms, admiration for audacity, loyalty, piety and disregard for personal safety. He is recorded to have carried out plenty of flamboyant knightly deeds as a young adult. He was very confident. A showman. He knew how to manipulate characteristics and traits that were appreciated by his contemporaries. He fought his first battle at the age of sixteen and from that point on became a prominent fighter as well as a leader in action. By the age of just ten, he knew how to ride, bend a bow, swim and hunt, later becoming an expert in all three.

Many knights were illiterate but we know Henry certainly was not. He had a good standard of education but, due to constantly being on the move, it was not as good as the educational elite. He was a great lover of music and by the same age could play the harp. He remained religiously devout. A Benedictine monk who was close to Henry in his youth testified to his punctuality in attending Mass and his weekly confessions. In fact, two issues which plagued Henry all his life was the Lollard (early Protestantism) movement and the Islamic occupation of the Holy land. He was a true product of his society in this respect which was intensely religious. As Peter Earle states, with Henry 'there was a tendency to swing from excessive worldliness to excessive piety...which was exaggerated by his showmanship'. The list of his religious foundations, donations to charity and the church was long and impressive. He did, however, sometimes take overtly excessive violent actions as J.R. Lander critically describes:

> There are more than hints of superstition and pride, even conceit, in Henry's piety. He dreaded the forces of witchcraft, yet like Constantine, even if unconsciously, he seems to have looked upon himself as something more than an ordinary child of God. So convinced of righteousness was he that religious opposition in particular drove him to furious vindictiveness. On the capture of Rouen, he imprisoned for life, in chains, the arch-bishop's vicar general who had excommunicated him during the course of the siege.

Also at Caen, during the siege, the French preacher St Vincent Ferrer, emphatically claimed in front of all, with a hooded face, that Henry could not be a man of God as he is oppressing Christ's people by war and devastation. After the victory, Henry rode up to the friar and told him 'I am the scourge of God sent to punish the people of God for their sins'. His extremely pious nature often instilled dread as much as inspiration.

Another revealing example of Henry's zeal of principles is displayed in the trial of one of his most intimate friends, Sir John Oldcastle, a Lollard leader accused of protecting and harboring heretics in the dioceses of London. Rather than have him customarily burned, Henry did his best to secure Sir John's submission and placed him in the tower of London for forty days to think it over. Before his accession, he supervised the burning of a Lollard Blacksmith in a barrel. When the Blacksmith began to scream, Henry personally pulled him out and offered him a pension if only he would recant. When the man refused Henry pushed him straight back in the barrel and nailed it shut. Ruthless authority and icy cruelty were interwoven characteristics of this king, perhaps necessary for such ruthlessly hard times, yet he also possessed great charisma and inspired genuine devotion.

Not all of his actions were so harsh. He knew how to make friends of his generals, friends who praised him for his generosity and loyalty. Politicians admired him for his courage and willingness to accommodate and to listen, and surviving letters are betrothed with evidence of his eagerness to help those around him. By late teens, he had learned to fight and lead. He knew what it was like to be wounded and to keep marching through the rain, wind and cold of winter. Despite being quite young, his interests in moral and theological questions were with him always and his hope to recover Jerusalem was a sign that he legitimately took his oaths at his coronation very seriously indeed. His physical appearance is rarely elaborated on, but what we do know is that he was fairly tall, slim build but wiry, deceptively strong, relatively good looking with a thin face and prominent features. E.F Jacob describes him as:

> A hard-bitten leader with experience of campaigning under conditions where the personal influence of the commander rather than the cash at his disposal was responsible for holding the troops together; a leader with a shrewd knowledge of men and an important following among the nobility. In person, Henry did not resemble a warrior. A Frenchman, Jean Fusoris ...observed that while the duke of Clarence really looked like a soldier, Henry had the fine manner of a Lord and noble stature, but seemed more suited to the church than to war.

Desmond Seward, author of 'A brief History of The hundred Years War', describes him as being 'tall and muscular, wearing his amour as though it were a light cloak. Under a brown pudding-basin crop – the military haircut of the day – he had brown eyes and a long nose in a long high colored face. In manner he was aloof but courteous. He had no mistresses, at least not when he was king'.

The reasons for Henry going to war are still vigorously debated at present. In gambling with half of his inheritance, some critics argue that there could never have been any doubt in his mind, resolute in his ambition to ascertain the other half. His royal cousin's possession of the kingdom of France was unjust and probably an insult to Henry and with France weakened by her domestic squabbles and feuding provinces as well as a lengthy relative period of peace between the two nations; war seemed an inevitable path with France. A war with France entailed other pleasantries. In the crudest fashion, it also meant plunder, excitement, adventure, and perhaps above all, glory. Before the reader judges Henry too quickly, one must not be too hasty in accusing him of war-mongering lest we forget this war was supported by Parliament and sanctioned by the church. As for the English nobility, referred to at the beginning of this chapter, warring with France was practically a way of life. Henry would have had no problems in gaining the support of the nobles, especially after a period of inactivity and deprivation of victory over the French. Out of seventeen members of the highest nobility in England, only three did not actively fight for the King during Henry's leadership. A closer look at Henry's character reveals traces of a deep insecurity and sense of self-doubt; behind his show-manship and aloof confidence, came hysterical insistences on his rights as King of England and almost fanatical claims of his close ties with the almighty. This can be linked to his fierce single-mindedness, such insecurity emanating from an unconscious recognition of the questionable nature in which he descended to the throne, only from a third son of Edward III; The Earl of March descending from a second son through the female line. In any case, there is an element of inevitability that

Henry V would gaze across the channel with burning desire to attack the House of Valois. Some argue that in doing so, Henry was strengthening and further uniting England in a common cause against the old enemy Le Bleu, thus diverting any unnecessary tension or activity at home against his own title. Keeping the nobles busy abroad would prevent them turning on each other at home. This was truly the beginning of a real cohesive English identity. Notably, as the Armagnac and Burgundy factions plunged France into chaos and disarray, one feels it would have been extremely difficult for any English king to show restraint and not seize the opportunity.

This leads us to the preparations of the famous 1415 campaign. Although England's population was significantly inferior, Henry did not appear to struggle in recruiting numbers for the campaign. Chroniclers and historians have previously embellished actual statistical information concerning numbers of fighting men, where in reality, research indicates that armies under Henry V never exceeded ten thousand soldiers; well under one percent of the nations' population. Henry, already possessing a renowned reputation for leading from the front and being a successful commander, no doubt contributed to the ease of filling the ranks of the army. The more successful a king was, the easier it became to find men to fight. England also had a reputation for recruiting criminals, as an outlaw serving for his king could mean a pardon and return to full citizenship. In some English armies of the fourteenth and fifteenth centuries, as much as five percent of the entire force consisted of murderers, rapists, thieves and vagabonds. Whether this be conceived an advantage or disadvantage is for the analyst to decide. During the period of 1414 and 1415 there was an enormous amount of activity up and down the country, with large quantities of materials, weapons, armor, siege equipment, livestock, wagons and bridging to name a few. Such operations were prepared by a series of loans and very generous contributions from the church and Parliament who unusually agreed to higher taxations on trade and estates, something the French King could only dream of. Even previous English Kings found such procurements exhaustingly difficult, yet Henry conspicuously managed to win over the establishments' authority; further reinforcing the argument of his exceptional and compelling unifying presence. Loans from Dick Whittington, John Hende, Bishop Beaufort and many abbots filled the war coffers.

The recruitment structure at the time was the indenture system; once captains confirmed the amount of men they could bring they then entered contracts of service with the King. This could range from ten or fifteen to hundreds of soldiers, often in a ratio of around three archers to one man-at-arms. The King would then pay the captains a quarter's wages in advance once they made their indentures. The next stage was the muster. It is here we see a revealing contrast in efficiency between Henry's administration and the opposing French. In the first place, Henry paying his soldiers in advance prevented his army from mirroring behavior and attitudes of the French, who from having to largely wait to be paid often had no choice but to live off pillage and plunder. Also, the excruciating efficiency of the English Mustering Officers would vigorously check that all the men were equipped with what was on the indenture specification from the captain. If men were missing parts of their armor, did not have enough arrows sheathed or were horseless, the bureaucratic Mustering Officers would deduct pay from the captains' wages. This ensured that captains did not try and cheat the Exchequer and were carrying out their part of the deal with the King. The organisation of English armies, compared to their many European counterparts, at the time, was more professional. The French, however, did employ captains (often called routiers) but in larger campaigns were heavily reliant on poorly trained feudal levies who were undisciplined. Such men had a reputation for embarrassing their leaders on the field and partly explain the fact that despite France's usual numerical advantage in terms of army size France usually lost major battles. The indentured battalions were not the only soldiers available to Henry. Ireland could always be relied on for conscripts as well as the elite royal household knights. Subjects abroad from Gascony and Aquitaine for example, also provided men on a par with England and had a reputation for being handy with a crossbow. Henry V went for quality, not quantity when it came to army strength. Above all, Henry believed that victory was not dependent on numbers but on God. Just like at Crecy and Poitiers seventy years or so earlier, where the French turned up in huge numbers on home soil yet suffered monumental defeats to the far smaller English armies. Research reveals that Henry, amidst his many talents had a real flair for logistics and personally oversaw the supply structure for the 1415 campaign from top to bottom.

A biography OF Henry V attributed with the most credibility is the 'Gesta Henrici Quinti', written by a priest in the king's chapel, between 1413 and 1416.

This contemporary royal scripter writes how Henry desired and attempted peace negotiations. He claimed that Henry was dedicated in achieving:

> ...those things which make for the honor of God, the extension of the Church, the freeing of his country and the tranquility of kingdoms, and especially of the two kingdoms of England and France that they might be more coherent and united, which from long and unhappy times past had damaged each other and caused deplorable effusion of human blood.

In treating these claims with objective suspicion, the reader is confronted with the question of how genuine any negotiations were on either the English or French side. Only at the Treaty of Troyes, between March and April 1420, did the French seriously attempt to negotiate as France was on her knees. The allegiance between England and Burgundy forced France into agreeing (on 9 April) Henry should marry Princess Catherine with a dowry of 40,000 crowns and that upon Charles VI's death; Henry should inherit the kingdom of France. Had Henry survived a few more months outliving the Dauphin, Charles VI, who died only months after Henry, France would have become legal and legitimate territory under English sovereignty indefinitely. It was only Henry's untimely death, on 31 August 1422, aged 35, that prevented him from achieving the impossible. After France, he would have no doubt set his sights on expelling the Muslim infidels from Jerusalem. As Desmond Seward succinctly states 'The Treaty of Troyes was one of the greatest humiliations in French History'.

Interestingly also pointed out is the fact that north of the river Loire, the treaty went uncontested by the people.

For the 1415 campaign, in total Henry raised an army of around 8000 archers and 2000 men-at arms. With everything in place, on Sunday 11 August 1415, Henry V with his fleet set sail on a war path to France which was to make our first protagonist one of the most famous and respected monarchs in history. Fifteen hundred ships were needed to haul the army, equipment and supplies across the channel. Henry V's confidence in victory is evidenced in his plan to conquer France with such a small army. Ten thousand troops seem small for any type of invasion by a ground assault, especially against superior numbers and wealth. Total colonisation would have taken many more numbers of troops and citizens which raises the question as to what Henry was trying to prove or achieve. Historians have noted that he was perhaps compelled to prove a point, a symbolic gesture that he could march into France unchallenged. Maybe he genuinely believed that with such a limited fighting force he could take on all what France had to offer, after all, English armies of the recent past had astonishing success on French soil. It is clear that he did not expect to be confronted with any sizable army waiting for him. Either way, what was probably intended initially as a full scale invasion turned out to be little more than a very successful raid, yet its significance led to a chain of events which ultimately resulted in the Treaty of Troyes. Apart from taking the harbour town of Harfleur, most of the damage (more of a psychological and spiritual nature) was inflicted at Agincourt. It was at the port of Harfleur that Henry did not have it all his own way. Due to well-fortified defences including three strong barbicans, twenty-six towers manned with several hundred men-at-arms and mounted canons together with strong drawbridges and a wide deep moat, commanded by a respected general – Sieur d'Estouteville, it took Henry five weeks and almost two thousand casualties to break this town. The worst enemy for the English army was not the French, but dysentery and malaria from contaminated water and poor camp conditions during the siege, claiming the lives of the Earls of Arundel, Suffolk, and March.

With winter fast approaching and a depleted army, marching further inland was out of the question. Many advisories insisted upon a return to England, however, Henry was not satisfied and decided on a 'chevauchee' all the way to Calais – some 160 miles from Harfleur. It is said that he 'was possessed of a very great desire of seeing his territories and had insisted on marching through Normandy to his other secure possession in northern France'. This was 160 miles of hostile territory; making this (as seen by many) to be a very strange decision - perceived almost as a suicide mission to some, however, as far as Henry was concerned the main French army was 150 miles away from Calais in Vernon. He would have a three day head start with a lighter, less encumbered and more disciplined force. The Dauphin's army had other ideas and decided to intercept the English with a force many times larger, gradually swelling with joining elements such as the Dukes of Alencon, Bourbon, Orleans and Brittany, all with many noble men-at-arms and prestigious knights itching for English blood. It is documented that the English at first were not aware of being followed until Henry tried to cross the river Somme only to find causeways and bridges destroyed and defended by thousands of French knights. Having to redirect along the Somme, with dwindling supplies, the cold October rain and marauding sporadic French skirmishes, the English army already suffering from dysentery and exhaustion, began to lose morale. With the river in flood, on 19 October, Henry managed to cross the Somme, beating off French harassing forces. The French appeared to have been in a position to attack, with odds in their favour, at any time yet seemed to have merely shadowed the English army without any meaningful confrontation. Some historians suggest this was down to a general incompetence of the French. Others insinuate that the French were determined, out of pride and chivalry, to wait and confront Henry in a full scale battle, as on 20 October, French heralds approached the English camp bearing a challenge stating:

> Our lords have heard how you intend with your army to conquer the towns, castles and cities of the realm of France and to depopulate French cities. And because of this and for the sake of their country and their oaths, many of our lords are assembled to defend their rights; and they inform you by us that before you come to Calais they will meet you to fight with you and be revenged of your conduct. (A Brief History of the Hundred Years war)

Henry, characteristically unfazed and not intimidated in the slightest, was reported to have replied 'be all things according to the will of God'.

The French did not reveal where they planned this confrontation but customs of the day indicated it would be a field which gave no real advantage to either side. The following day, while the English trudged on, covering as much as eighteen miles a day through dreadful weather towards Calais, the French made a disastrous decision in marching out of Peronne where they were based (space where they had abundant room to manoeuvre their huge army), and proceeded to cut across the path of the English and intercept Henry. Upon sight of such an 'innumerable host of locusts', all hope of retreat had faded, as the English slumped up the hill towards the village of Maisoncelles. The events which ensued no doubt will echo through eternity in English history, and to pay homage and give rightful justice, rather than provide a personal interpretation, the following is a substantial extract taken from Douglas and Myers 'English Historical Documents' and is an actual eyewitness account of the battle of Agincourt.

The battle of Agincourt, according to an eye-witness, 1415 (Henrici Quinti Angliae Regis Gesta, ed. B Williams (English Historical society, 1850), 44-60 [Latin]

And when on the following day, Thursday, we were descending the valley towards the river of the swords, the king was told by scouts and cavalry skirmishers that there was a powerful adversary numbering many thousands on the other side of the river, almost a league to our right. We therefore crossed the river as fast as we could, and when we reached the crest of the hill on the other side, we saw emerging from the valley about a mile from us hateful swarms of Frenchman, who appeared to us to be an incomparable multitude in their columns, lines and divisions. They took up their position just over half a mile ahead of us, filling a broad field like an innumerable swarm of locusts, having a small valley between us and them.

Meanwhile our king was encouraging his army courteously and bravely, marshalling them into lines and wings, as if they were to go at once into battle. And then everyone who had not previously cleared his conscience by confession, put on the armour of penitence...And among other sayings which I noted then, a certain knight, Sir Walter Hungerford, wished to the king's face that in addition to the small band which he had there he could have had ten thousand of the better archers of England, who would have been glad to be with them. The king replied: "Thou speakest a fool, for by the God of heaven in whose grace I trust and in whom is my firm hope of victory, I would not have one more than I have, even if I could...Dost thou not believe that the almighty can through this humble little band overcome the pride of these Frenchmen, who boast of their numbers and their strength?"...

And when the enemy in position saw and considered the disposition and fewness of our troops, they betook themselves to a field beyond a certain wood, which lay near to the left between us and them, where was our road to Calais. So our king, thinking that they might go round the wood to attack him along the road, or else thinking that they might go round woods further away in the neighbourhood and surround us from all sides, at once moved his lines as he always stationed himself to face the enemy...

And when at last we were at the last rays of light, and darkness fell between us and them, we still stood in the field and heard our foes, everyone calling as the manner is, for his comrade, servant and friend, dispersed by chance in so great a multitude. Our men began to do the same, but the king ordered silence throughout the whole army, under penalty of the loss of horse and harness in the case of a gentleman...and the right of ear in the case of a yeoman or below, with no hope of pardon, for anyone who might presume to break the king's order. And he at once went in silence to a hamlet nearby, in a place where we had only a few houses; most of us had to rest in gardens and orchards, through a night of pouring rain. And when our enemies considered the quietness of our men and our silence, they thought that we were struck with fright at our small numbers and contemplated flight during the night; so they established fires and strong watches throughout the fields and routes. And as it was said they thought they were so sure of us that they cast dice that night for our king and nobles.

And on the morrow, Friday the feast of Saints Crispin and Crispinian, 25th October, the Frenchmen, at dawn, organised themselves into lines, battles, and wedges, and took up there position facing us in the field called Agincourt, through which lay our route to Calais, in terrific multitude; and they set squadrons of horsemen in many hundreds on either side of their front lines, to break our line and the strength of our archers. The front line was composed of dismounted men made up of all the noblest and choicest of their forces, who in the forest of spears...were by estimation thirty times more numerous than our men. But their rear lines...were all on horseback...and compared with our men they were an innumerable multitude.

And meanwhile our king prepared himself for the field, after hearing lauds and masses and...arranged his small numbers in one "battle", placing his vanguard as a wing to his right with the Duke of York in command and the rearguard as a wing to his left under Lord Camoys. Interspersed among the line were wedges of archers, whom the king ordered to affix stakes in front of them, as he had ordered earlier, to stop the attacks of the horsemen...

And when much of the day had been consumed...and both armies had stood and had not moved a foot, the king, seeing that the opposing army was abstaining from the attack which had been expected...either to cause us to break our order, or to strike terror into our hearts because of their numbers...ordered his men to move towards the enemy, sending orders to the baggage train to follow up so that they should not fall as booty to the enemy. After the king had estimated that all his baggage had come up to his rear, he advanced towards the enemy, with his men, in the name of Jesus...and of the glorious virgin and St George, and the enemy moved towards him.

And when they came near enough to attack, the French horsemen posted on the sides rushed against our archers on both flanks of our army; but quickly, God willing, they were compelled to retreat by the showers of arrows and to flee behind their lines...except the large numbers whom the points of the stakes or the sharpness of the arrows stopped from flight by piercing the horses or horsemen. The crossbowmen of the enemy, who were behind the men at arms and on their flanks, fell back in face of the strength of our archers after the first draw, which was too hasty and injured only a few of our men...but the French nobles who had first approached in line, just as they had come from their muster nearby...divided themselves into three columns, *either for fear of the arrows...or to penetrate more quickly our force to the banners, attacked our forces at the three places where there were banners; and at the first clash they met our men with such a fierce impact that they were compelled to fall back for almost the distance of a lance...And then the battle grew hotter and our archers shot...their arrows through the flanks of the enemy, the battle continually renewing. And when our arrows were exhausted, they seized axes, swords and lances from those who were lying on the ground, and beat down, wounded and killed the enemy with them...And the just judge who wished to strike down the proud multitude of the enemy with the thunderbolts of vengeance...broke their power...No one had time to receive them as captives, but almost all of them without distinction of persons, when they fell to the ground, struck down by our men, I know not by what hidden judgement of God, were killed without intermission...For when some of them slain at the start of the engagement fell in front, such was the undisciplined violence and pressure of the host behind that the living fell on the dead, and others falling on the living were killed in turn; and so in the three places where there was a concentration of our forces, the piles of dead and those crushed in between grew so much that our men climbed on these heaps which grew higher than a man and slew those below with swords, axes and other weapons. And when at last after two or three hours the vanguard was cut up and worn out, and the rest were forced into flight, our men began to sort these heaps and separate the living from the dead, intending to keep the living as property to be ransomed. But behold! At once, we know not by what wrath of God, a cry arose that the* enemy's rear guard of cavalry, in overwhelming numbers had repaired the enemy line...and was coming against our small and tired band. And so they killed their prisoners with swords...without any distinction of persons, except for the Dukes of Orleans and Bourbon and other illustrious persons in the royal entourage, and a few others, less the captives should be our ruin in the coming battle.

But after a little while, the troops of the enemy, having tasted the bitterness of our weapons, and at our king's approach, left the field of blood to us, by God's will, with carts and many other waggons filled with victuals, and spears, lances and bows...

Of the French there were according to their own enumeration more than 60,000 bearing the sword, whereas the number of our small company of fighters did not exceed 6,000 men. Of this multitude there fell the Dukes of Bar, Brabant, and Alencon, five counts, more than 90 barons and bannerets, whose names are given in the book of records, and more than 1500 knights, according to their own computation, and between 4000 and 5000 other gentle folk, almost the whole nobility of French chivalry...But there was great joy amongst our people and great astonishment, because of our small forces there were found dead on the field not more than nine or ten persons, beyond the illustrious Lord Edward Duke of York and the Lord Michael, Earl of Suffolk...and two newly created knights. Therefore our England has cause for joy and cause for grief; for joy because of a great victory and the salvation of our men, for grief because of the suffering and death of Christians.

And one cannot recall...that any prince ruled...more industriously, vigorously or humanely his people or *acted in a more manly fashion on the field of battle; it is not recorded in chronicles or annals of the realm, in which our past is recorded, that any king of England ever accomplished so much in so short a time, and returned to his own realm with so great and glorious a triumph. To God alone be the honour and glory, world without end. Amen.* (pg 210-214)

In just over half an hour, the battle was more or less decided. After that point it nolonger became a matter of whether the French would lose but of how bad the damage would be. It is said the French were consumed and blurred by so much hate for their adversaries that day, but the English were filled with blood-lust and had their wits about them. The mindless mass charge by the French nobility no doubt played right into English hands. Henry's death squad of 200 archers did most of the dirty work, slaughtering the wounded and prisoners, preserving only the super-rich. Most of the heavy fighting was conducted round the king himself, as French knights took turns trying to reach him. Henry's true lionhood comes from his actions on the field with his men, toe to toe with the enemy, personally distinguishing himself in the battle and even saving his brother Humphrey. It is unknown how many knights the king defeated singlehandedly, but an educated guess would suggest it was double figures. The total roll of dead at Agincourt is undetermined as nobody thought to count those of a lower class who died.

At Agincourt, against all expectation, the English defeated a much larger and stronger French army on French soil. In arguably England's greatest military victory, the immobility and lack of true leadership in the French army cost France almost her sovereignty.

Quite often throughout history, it is England that's left wanting in men of great influence to follow, but under Henry V rule there was no absence of leadership. Agincourt was a fantastic achievement against near impossible odds. The battle concreted the reputation of Henry as a fighting warrior king almost overnight. His prestige in France elevated to such levels that never again did a French force attempt to engage him in a traditional battle. It is true, however, that the Agincourt campaign, with the exception of Harfleur, brought little other than fame and glory. Much of France was still out of his control, and while many French lay dead and Henry reflected on the future, new French armies were being raised. Had there not been such a deep division between the Armagnacs and Burgundy in France, Henry would have probably thought twice. Under Henry V, the Hundred Years War developed into a national struggle for Englishmen and Frenchmen alike. Importantly the English Gentry stopped speaking French completely and unquestionably the antagonism between medieval Englishmen and Frenchmen represented a genuine mutually experienced national xenophobia. English and French identity and culture was in its infancy, both carving out their respective characters yet continually locked in binary opposition. By the period of Joan of Arc, the term *'Godon'* – 'God-damn' was used frequently to describe an Englishman. A French writer at the time conveyed perhaps an accurate description of French feelings towards the English:

> The war they have waged and still wage is false, treacherous and damnable, but then they are an accursed race, opposed to all good and all reason,

ravening wolves, proud arrogant hypocrites, tricksters without any conscience, tyrants and persecutors of Christians, men who drink and gorge on human blood, with natures like birds of prey, people who live only by plunder.

Perhaps the truth is the French and English are closer than what they like to admit. During this period, the only difference was Henry V. In the summer of 1422 he became very ill and was unable to ride. After fulfilling part of the treaty of Troyes, in marrying princess Catherine who it is claimed he was madly in love with, they had a child; Henry VI. Approaching close to death, with his organisational thoroughness, he appointed his brother, Bedford as Regent of France and protectorate of the baby Henry VI, and Gloucester was made Regent of England. He proclaimed to the end that his invasion of France was to bring about a lasting peace between the two peoples. He died peacefully at Vincennes on 31 August 1422, aged 35.

Timeline of King Henry V

Key events

1413 – 1422 King Henry V reigned as King of England from March 21, 1413 - August 31, 1422

1387 – Henry was born on September 16, 1387 in Monmouth, Wales, he was known as Prince Hal. Henry was the son of King Henry IV (1367-1413) and Mary de Bohun (c. 1369-1394)

1400 – King Henry IV quashed the Welsh rebellion led by Owain Glyndwr who had declared himself Prince of Wales with the help of Prince Hal

1403 – The Battle of Shrewsbury was fought on July 21, 1403: The Battle of Shrewsbury where King Henry quashed the rebellion of Henry Percy, 1st Earl of Northumberland (Harry Hotspur) once again with the help of Prince Hal

1405 – King Henry IV suffered from an unnamed illness and suffered recurring illnesses up to his death

1410 – The health of King Henry IV was so bad that his son, Prince Hal, took over many of his kingly duties

1413 – March 20, 1413: King Henry IV died in Westminster and was buried at Canterbury Cathedral

1413 – 9 April 1413: The coronation of King Henry V

1415 – Southampton Plot: Henry quashed the Southampton plot which was in favour of Mortimer

1415 – The Siege of Harfleur: Henry invaded France and gained a victory at the Siege of Harfleur. The town surrendered on 22 September

1415 – 25 October 1415 the Battle of Agincourt: One of the greatest victories in the Hundred Years War against France, famous for the English use of the Longbow

1420 – Treaty of Troyes: Henry was recognised by the French in the Treaty of Troyes as heir to the French throne. This was cemented by his marriage to Catherine of Valois, the daughter of King Charles VI.

1420 – June 2, 1420: Henry married Catherine of Valois (27 October 1401 – 3 January 1437), the daughter of King Charles VI, thus cementing the Treaty of Troyes

1421 – 6 December 1421: The only child of Catherine and Henry was born was referred to as Henry of Windsor (who later became King Henry VI)

1422 – August 31, 1422: King Henry V died of dysentery at Bois de Vincennes. He was buried in Westminster Abbey

1422 – King Henry V was succeeded by his son who became King Henry VI

1429 – Catherine of Valois secretly married a Welsh courtier called Owen Tudor after the death of King Henry V - they became the grand parents of King Henry VII of England.

CHAPTER 4

Oliver Cromwell:
The Lord Protector of England.

Lord, I may, I will come to thee for thy people. Thou hast made me, though very unworthy, a mean instrument to do them some good and thee service; and many of them have set too high a value upon me, though others wish and would be glad of my death. Lord, however thou dost dispose of me, continue and go on to do good for them...Teach those who look too much on thy instruments to depend more upon thyself. Pardon such as desire to trample upon the dust of a poor worm, for they are thy people to.

(Oliver Cromwell – his death came minutes after reciting).

No other Englishman has had the ability to divide a nation, even to this day; Oliver Cromwell creates deep rooted controversy. From a traditional family that owed its status to the reformation, tutored by a puritan school master and attending the highly puritan Sidney Sussex College of the University of Cambridge, Cromwell could only gravitate in one direction. Sidney Sussex College was perhaps the most puritan of all the colleges at the time, where from 1610 to 1643 the Master of the college was the renowned Calvinist, Samuel Ward. His existence and presence of voice intensified hostility towards popery in the church, and eventually, the king himself. In April 1615 he was sent to college only to return a year later due to the death of his father, Robert Cromwell. There is no evidence to suggest Oliver ever returned to complete his scholarly pursuits. Cromwell had a humble childhood growing up in East Anglia, a modest family in comparison to many of his contemporaries. In fact, Oliver had numerous wealthy and powerful relatives. After his father's death, in 1620, Oliver married Elizabeth Bouchier, the daughter of a success-ful merchant from London, who also happened to be a distant relation to Cromwell's cousins in Essex. It is plain to see that such a marriage edged him closer to those who would become the opposing collective at the helm of the parliamentary opposition. Although a poor relation in many ways, it is well documented that Cromwell was in touch with some of the more influential families in England. His connections inevitably acted as a significant factor in his political and military end-eavours. Some of the names Oliver was connected to include the Knightleys, the Gerrards, the Hampdens, the St Johns, the Hammonds, the Waltons and the Hobarts. When Oliver was first elected in the House of Commons in 1628, he discovered eight or nine cousins there.

During the early stages of the revolution, parlia-ment abolished the Prerogative Courts, the Council of the North and the High Commission simultaneously declaring that all taxation without parliament's consent was illegal. Long Parliament was declared indissoluble except by its own consent, Bishops were expelled from the House of Lords and the Archbishop, Laud, incarcerated in the Tower of London.

There were popish conspiracies floating around of which such fear manifested in the removal and destruction of altar rails, communion tables and painted glass often with violent and meaningful disrespect. The Irish rebellion in October 1641was the final tipping point, inducing the first whisperings of Charles' gross misconduct in office. Parliament brought before the House an exhaustive list of all charges that could be brought against Charles' government over the last ten years. Such an unprecedented event diachronically divided the nation in two. After an embarrassing failure by Charles to arrest the most vocal in the house, civil war broke out in 1642. At the rank of colonel, in May 1643, under orders from Essex, Cromwell moved into Lincoln-shire expected to be joined by other commanders of the cause, which in turn, could support General Fairfax who was greatly under pressure and threatened with attack by Royalists in Yorkshire. However, no other support arrived, and so, true to character, Cromwell acted alone. When he reached Grantham, he discovered a Royalist contingent three times larger than his own force. With-out hesitation and aware of his inferiority in numbers, he led the charge. The enemy, shocked by such daring and bravery, turned and fled. This incident at Grantham was amongst the first where Cromwell acted as an inde-pendent commander and became a typical occurrence of his 'lead from the front' behaviour.

After the close fought defeat at Edgehill, certain parliamentarians began to waver and question the achievability of warring against the king. The Earl of Manchester's infamous argument put forward to the House, increased parliamentary division and allowed political space for Cromwell to raise his voice. Manchester's argument was 'If we beat the king ninety nine times yet he still be our king, and so will his posterity be after him; but if the king beat us once, we shall all be hanged...'. Cromwell responded with 'my Lord, if this be so, why did we take up arms at first? This is against fighting ever hereafter...' Not only was this an ideological clash of perceptions of the war, but a conflict over the very axioms of going to war. Cromwell desperately felt the urgency to end Charles' theft, neglect and systematic abuse of his English subjects whereas Manchester was still infected by the dogmatism and hypocrisy of a Parliamentarian Royalist, procrastinating tediously for as long as possible. Manchester accused Cromwell of being disobedient to authority and the king, to which Cromwell, with his patriotic rhetoric hit back with a persuasive speech to the House:

> Without a more speedy, vigorous and effective prosecution of the war...we shall make the kingdom weary of us, and hate the name of parliament...waving a strict enquiry into the causes of these things, let us apply ourselves to the remedy. And I hope we have such true English hearts and zealous affection towards the general weal of our mother country as no member of either House will scruple to deny themselves, and their own private interests, for the public good, nor account it to be a dishonour

done to them, whatever the parliament shall
resolve upon in this weighty matter.

Upon analysis, these are the words of not just a patriot,
but of a soldier and a statesman, a true leader in the
making who was aware of the problems of parliament
and the contempt of the monarch. As contemporary
readers, we would do well to remember that the majority of the population, at this time was still Royalist at
heart, still vigorously attached to their churches and its
doctrines, ultimately the king of course being head of
the faith. In attempting to understand Oliver's audacious
achievements, one must wonder how he managed almost
singlehandedly (at least in the House of Commons) to
interpolate such an influential wave of puritanism,
leading to the abolition of bishops in parishes, wide-
spread condemnation of catholic idolatry and an uneasy
aggression towards all other denominations seen as
straying from the straight path. As discoveries unfold,
one could effortlessly gravitate to the assumption that
considering the collective social conscience of the period,
Cromwell's achievements are difficult to measure.

Around early January 1657, parliament began the
debate on how to form a new government. Much to
Cromwell's confusion, this included offering him the
title of king and the formation of two Houses of
Parliament - the remnants of Westminster to this day,
the House of Commons and the House of Lords.
Research informs us that officials attempted to persuade
Oliver to accept the throne, a sentiment widely accepted
by parliament and the population. We can infer it was
a difficult decision for Cromwell. His concerns were
primarily the security and prosperity of the state but

also the impact of such a decision on puritanism itself. He was aware that the protestant faith would perceive any acceptance of the throne in a hypocritical and treacherous light and puritanism, God's people, would suffer as a consequence. Therefore, in 1657, Oliver Cromwell, after liberating the English nation form tyranny, refused to accept the title of king and remained humble protector of the realm. Cromwell addressed the two Houses and warned 'if you run into another flood of blood and war, the sinews of this nation being wasted by the last, it must sink and perish utterly'. His words fell on deaf ears as documents inform us that within a year the new government had so quickly and shamefully deteriorated. On the 4th February 1658, Cromwell hired a coach and drove straight to Westminster where he congregated both Houses. Shortly before accusing them of exactly what the king was found guilty of the year before, he reminded them not only that an immovable obnoxious parliament is more insulting than an obnoxious king, but also that:

> I would have been glad as to my own conscience
> and spirit to have been living under a Woodside,
> and to have kept a flock of sheep, rather than
> to have undertaken such a place as this…But
> I undertook it for the safety of the nation

With that, he dismissed both Houses. That same year, on Friday 3rd September, Oliver Cromwell slipped gently into that good night, minutes after he recited the prayer quoted at the beginning of this chapter.

It could be argued that once the war was underway, Charles was always going to struggle to maintain a credible effort as the richest counties of the day – Yorkshire, East Anglia, Lancashire, the Home Counties and London all largely supported parliament. Cromwell had a financial advantage, as long as he could unify the army. The king's weakness was that his aristocracy possessed very little fighting experience, due to the relative peace and tranquil reign of Elizabeth I. To make things worse for Charles, any hint of employing catholic armies from Ireland, Scotland (highlanders only) or Europe would have, and did, alienate him further from the larger classes of England. There were occasions when Charles flirted, and even concocted draft proposals for an invading catholic force. Before the king had chance to fulfil his treacherous ambition, the morale and enthusiasm of Cromwell's lower class protestants increased eight fold as Oliver snatched victory at the battle of Naseby on 14 June 1645. Oliver's tempestuous and insolent manner in defence of the commoners attracted significant notice by his peers; as did his sartorial discrepancies, as noticed by Sir Philip Warwick, who described Oliver as wearing 'a plain cloth suit, which seemed to have been made by an ill country tailor'. However humble Cromwell's image, his lacking prestige and elegance did not detract from his power and influence in the House or on the field. Although Naseby did not mark the finality of the war, it certainly demarcates the sharp and irrecoverable decline of Charles' reign.

What remains of the upmost importance, is the fact that the English revolution, unlike the French and Russian revolutions, had no previous similar comparison to draw upon. The French revolution could peer back at the English example almost two hundred years before; the Russian revolution could look back at both. Neither

was it reinforced and supported by any radical revolutionary ideology, no Rousseau, Hobbes or Karl Marx
inspiring intellectual ideology or theoretical revolutionary changes. There was a vacuum of aspiring future
ideas such as liberty, equality, fraternity. The English
revolution was not about the dawn of some icono-
clastic concept, but rather about holding on to what the
English had, mostly God, religion, freedom and property.
If there were any ideological foundations behind the
revolution, it surely emanated through its greatest
advocate, Oliver Cromwell. He took it upon himself
to defend the protestant faith against Roman popery
and protect the middle classes from losing property to
the king. This aside, there was no real concrete and
established theory, just a belief that all wrongs committed
by the king and his 'evil councillors', papists and bishops
were due to feel the Lord's wrath. So when thousands of
Englishmen surprisingly found themselves in the context
of a revolution and unwillingly forced to make a choice
in many cases, they were ill-equipped to make a decision.
They simply had to improvise, thus what was waiting
and readily available was the holy Bible, which had been
in circulation in English translation for the last hundred
years. People had always been encouraged to read the
good book as the main source of knowledge and all its
wisdom. The place where answers can be obtained.

Contrary to the belief of many, despite Oliver's
devout protestant convictions, he advocated that truth is
to be found in the plurality of doctrines, in a multitude
of beliefs, as Christopher Hill accurately credits Oliver:

Cromwell – and it is one of his very great
contributions to English history – clung

tenaciously to this belief that truth was not
certainly possessed by any one sect. He never
expressed himself more forcefully than when
he besought the Scottish Presbyterians to think
it possible that they might be mistaken. This
helps to explain Oliver's patience in discussions
with men who profoundly disagreed with
him...He drew the line of course, at Catholics
and Episcopalians, for he held the mass to be
idolatrous...and in his view were repressive
systems which might prevent Christian verity
from expressing itself.

It may be fair to say, with particular consideration for
the Irish, that Cromwell's tolerance levels were much
higher to creeds in England than during his conquests of
the home nations. There is a very strong, tangible sense
that the existence of predestination lying at the heart
of Protestantism, acted as a spiritual catalyst driving
Cromwell's steely determination. Luther captures the
resonance and essence of the puritan position:

For if you doubt, or disdain to know that God
foreknows and wills all things, not contingently
But necessarily and immutably, how can you
believe confidently, trust and depend upon his
Promises...For without predestination, Christian
faith is utterly destroyed, and the promises of
God and the whole gospel entirely fall to the
ground...For the greatest and only consolation
of Christians in their adversities is the knowing
that God lies not but does all things immutably,

and that his will cannot be resisted, changed
or hindered.

The puritans, including Cromwell, believed in divine
grace, which not only differentiated them from everyone else but made them work hard to consciously glorify
God. The psychological advantages of such a trait to a
group from the masses were profound.

The Catholics in 1646 attempted to anger and frust-
rate puritan forces in England by claiming Cromwell
propagated the motto:

> Whate'er the popish hands have built
> Our hammers shall undo
> We'll break their pipes and burn their copes
> And pull down their churches too

There is no evidence this came from Cromwell. In
fact, after the battle of Edgehill (Cromwell and
Manchester's first significant defeat), Oliver recognised
the importance of a disciplined and orderly army and
such petty slandering would seem way out of character
and beneath Cromwell's integrity. Such accusations did
not appear to have distracted him, if anything, merely
added to his stoicism. This was a man who promulgated
the most daring and boldest gesture in history – the
beheading of a monarch by his own subjects, the first in
Europe's modern history.

There are contrasting historical accounts of the
reputation of Cromwell's men. In August 1642, as the
king began reinforcing his barracks at Nottingham,
Oliver initiated the raising of a cavalry regiment at
Huntingdon, which by later the following year, became

to be known as the famous 'Ironsides'. In defence of the liberty of the gospel and law of the land, it is generally agreed that Oliver's men were carefully picked soldiers – 'men, who upon a matter of conscience engaged in this quarrel'. After the defeat of Edgehill back in October 1642, Cromwell learnt a valuable lesson facing the quality ranks of the king's nobles and their sons beside them, matching them only with 'old, decayed serving men without honour, courage and resolution'. Cromwell is also reported to have said to Manchester 'you must get men of spirit...that is likely to go on as far as gentlemen will go, or else I am sure you will be beaten still'. From this point on, Oliver's men stood firm with the sword in one hand and the bible grasped firmly in the other.

One of many descriptions of Cromwell's Ironsides, is of men 'having been industrious and active in their former callings...afterwards finding the sweet of good pay, and of opulent plunder, the lucrative part made gain seem to them a natural member of Godliness'. Another account suggests 'these men were of greater understanding than common soldiers...they were the more engaged to be valiant'. Most accounts agree that Oliver enforced strict discipline on his men, added to the fact that a prerequisite to get into the Ironsides was a zealous belief in the gospel and men worthy of the title 'Godly'. A renowned quote from Cromwell compounds such assumptions:

> I had rather had a plain russet-coated captain that knows what he fights for and loves what he knows than what you call a gentleman and nothing else... If you choose honest, Godly men to be captains of horse, honest men will follow them...a few honest men are better than numbers.

It was such leadership of good men, that in July 1644, it became decisive at the battle of Marston Moor, where the parliamentarians didn't just win but dismantled the Royalist army which culminated in severely demoralising the king's camp. Up until this point, Marston Moor was the biggest battle ever to be fought on British soil. The ruthless 'psalm-singing' general Cromwell led the most ferocious charge that day, that all of England's ancestors felt the 'will reverberating in the earth'. With staggering pride, scout Leonard Watson, attached to Oliver's Ironsides, emphatically claimed 'we came down the hill in the bravest order and with the greatest resolution that ever was seen', straight into Prince Rupert's elite unit of royal horse, which in turn, attempted a counter-charge that only just failed. Fairfax, a loyal commander of the parliamentarian forces, also repeatedly fought bravely that day, being surrounded at one point, 'cutting and hacking' himself to safety, meeting Cromwell on the field. Research shows that Rupert's army, combined with Lord Newcastle's forces from York, numbered around nineteen thousand men, combined with the advantage of ground, holding a strong defensive position and strategically advantageous deployment of their cavalry. The parliamentarians amassed a deployment of some twenty six thousand men but with a distinct terrain disadvantage. According to investigations conducted by Sir Charles Firth and Christopher Hill, for more than three hours the two opposing armies stood facing each other. The roundheads emotionally resorted to singing psalms, giving the Royalists the impression that confrontation was unlikely, until the parliamentarians eventually began to advance, led from the front by Cromwell. Oliver's stoicism was evident in abundance on the battlefield, being wounded in the neck and becoming nearly totally blind by a firearms wound yet he refused to leave the field and stayed with his men. If actions indeed carry more signification than words, then the battle of Marston Moor epitomises the valour, bravery and devotion of Oliver Cromwell. Such attributes that so many critics both in the seventeenth century and presently refute and deny with vigour. It was at Marston Moor where Prince Rupert (who was captured and taken prisoner) found new appreciation for his psalm-singing roundhead enemy. It was Rupert, who after the battle, gave Cromwell the nickname 'Ironside', consequently spreading to his personal regiment – the Ironsides. In one of Cromwell's letters regarding this battle, he gives a brief account of what happened:

England and the church of God hath had a great favour from the Lord in this great victory given unto us, such as the like never was since this war began. It had all the the evidences of an absolute victory, obtained by the Lord's blessing upon the Godly party principally...The left wing, which I commanded, being our own horse, beat all the prince's horse...God made them as stubble to our swords...We routed all we charged I believe of twenty thousand the Prince hath not four thousand left. Give glory, all the glory, to God

As well as beneficial economic factors in favour of the parliamentarians (as mentioned earlier), an argument must be put forward for the psychological advantages the revolutionaries clearly had, largely facilitated by

Oliver himself. Through enigmatically powerful rhetoric, Cromwell incandescently generated the demarcation line – either cooperate with the king or cooperate with God. Such a cognitive alignment with omnipotence in adversity against a tyrant and traitor to his subjects, sent Cromwell's follower's morale to a level that 'even if the enemy had numbered all the grains of sand on the earth', victory was still assured. Oliver himself said 'I could not but smile out to God in praises in assurance of victory, because God would, by things that are not, bring to naught things that are…And God did it'. Puritanism's simple and humble values (indirectly compared to Catholicism) convincingly gave the revolutionaries internal and psychological strength, enabling puritan fighters to be released from fear and dread of damnation or failure, blessing them to fight with confidence, to fight alone if needed. It was this empowering of the individual which allowed Protestantism to change England forever and give birth to the individualist society we have today. Cromwell and the puritans, freed from collective mass, communion and confession, from golden crosses, idols of Mary and luxurious silk – to a life emphasising hard work, humility and complete individual trust in God alone.

Puritanism roused Englishmen from Catholicism's dogmatic slumber through teaching courage and mental strength, enforcing rationality not superstition. It became in many ways, an antidote to Catholicism's infectious cultural decay, and as Christopher Hill so eloquently articulates:

Puritanism overthrew the doctrine of passive obedience to divinely constituted authority. The

puritan theory appeals to human willpower and
to some degree human reason; not to arbitrary
divine intervention from outside

The religious hysteria surrounding the revolution would
suggest, deceivingly, the civil war was mainly religious
in nature. This is not the case. Protestantism was
established in 1559 and was very much a part of the
national identity, however, what was real was the feeling
that this very identity was being subverted from above.
Catholicism was not a rival but more of a threat.
Concerns were exacerbated in the awareness that the
queen, Henrietta Maria, was catholic and had a large
papist contingent around her in court. Such an influence
so close to the throne, it was bound to have an impact
on Charles, so when William Laud was made archbishop
of Canterbury, predestinarian teaching outlawed at
educational institutes and the reintroduction of greater
popery ceremonial church services, the English protestant was going to react unfavourably. Cromwell was
highly tuned in to the feelings of the commoners.

For those critics who doubt Oliver Cromwell's
motives, for those who accuse him of warmongering, the
following quote, in his speech to the Commons in
December 1644, reveal Cromwell's disdain for the
conflict and the suffering it brought to the people; a
quote which also highlights his profound political skills
that match his robust military command:

It is now time to speak, or forever hold the
tongue. The important occasion now is no less
than to save a nation out of a bleeding, nay,
almost dying condition, which the long

continuance of this war hath already brought it into; so that without a more speedy, vigorous and effectual prosecution of the war – casting off all lingering proceedings like soldiers of fortune beyond sea...For what do the enemy say? Nay, what do many say that were friends at the beginning of this parliament? Even this, that the members of both Houses have got great places and commands, and the sword, into their hands; and, what by interest in the parliament, what by power in the army, will perpetually continue themselves in grandeur, and not permit the war speedily to end, lest their own power should determine with it. This I speak here to our own faces is but what others do utter abroad behind our backs. I am far from reflecting on any. I know the worth of those commanders, members of both Houses, who are yet in power; but if I may speak my conscience without reflection upon any, I do conceive if the army be not put into another method, and the war more vigorously prosecuted, the people can bear the war no longer, and will enforce you to a dishonourable peace

After this speech, Cromwell immediately offered to resign his military position. Essex and Manchester were decommissioned but Oliver kept his command. So contagious was Cromwell's energy in the House, that in 1652 he persuaded parliament to pass on an act of pardon for all 'treasons committed' before the battle of Worcester (where Royalists behaved appallingly before the battle). An act of political expediency, or, as some cynics believed, an attempt to selfishly consolidate his own political position? Such critics have committed the most erroneous and gravest fallacy in questioning the sincerity of Cromwell's words. His legacy is deeply rooted to the notion that free men motivated by genuine conviction in their belief that superior morale and discipline would triumph over professionals. Oliver's soldiers were originally handpicked, well paid, adequately equipped and well versed in tactics. This is precisely the distinguishing difference between himself and his contemporaries, as he was able to use his cavalry charge to devastating effect. The king's cavalry would charge with great success but often one charge was all they managed due to loss of cohesion induced by immediate plundering and chasing individual routers. Cromwell's Ironsides could simply charge, rally, and recharge all day long. Even when suspected defeat hovered above them, still they would stand ground, ready for new orders. Not through physical or weapon superiority did this difference lie, but in superior discipline and morale forged on the belief that those who act to help themselves shall in turn be helped by God.

Unfortunately since Cromwell, mistaken impressions of the Lord Protector as a despotic autocrat, a tyrant, and in one case (embarrassingly), 'the English devil', have surfaced from their ignorant origins. If one digs deep enough through the annals of bygone written work, absurd comparisons with Hitler, Mussolini and Stalin have regrettably and woefully been made. The very idea of Cromwell as a tyrannical protector imposing a totalitarian dictatorship is categorically and fundamentally inaccurate. Allowing room for some subjectivity, it nonetheless remains extremely difficult to sustain an image of Cromwell (knowing what we know) as an autocratic, ruthless military dictator. First of all, the majority of the terms laid out in both constitutions by parliament, restricted the Lord Protector in terms of power far more than a monarch ruling with a council and parliament. More specifically, Oliver lacked the functions and logistics enabling him to behave as a dictator. With the absence of any bureaucracies, a professional police force or political group, and his isolation from most of the Lords of the land, enforcing his will would have proved very difficult. What he did have was the loyalty of the army (which he gradually decommissioned) and influence on the church. The way to people's hearts was always through the church. Such influence was never abused; Cromwell's piety, humility and zeal of the protestant faith can seldom be questioned. There is no room for doubt, that Oliver Cromwell took his protectoral oath 'to govern these nations according to the laws, statutes and customs thereof' extremely seriously. Another fact for Cromwell's critics is that under his protectorate, no one was executed for any political transgressions other than high treason. The author, G.E.Seel, in *The English Wars and Republic 1637-1660*, articulates this point succinctly:

> It is impossible to perceive Cromwell as being driven forward by an ideology that necessitated the formation of a dictatorship, even if that had been possible given the circumstances of the times. Instead, he was much more concerned to provide liberty to tender consciences and to heal

and settle the nation...and that the monarchy should not be resurrected- not because he himself might yet enjoy more power as Lord Protector, but because monarchy was an institution against which God had judged....time and time again he appears fearful of the authority that he possessed

The difficulty and almost impossible nature of Cromwell's position is expressed by John Morrill in his introduction to *Revolution and Restoration*:

Cromwell was endlessly torn between seeing the revolution as being a liberation of the people of God – the saints – and a call to the English nation as a new chosen race

However, Morrill also goes on to say that the Lord Protector's cause became 'exhausted and disillusioned'. With these statements in mind, one must remember that Cromwell's great achievements (political, militarily and religious) were packed into just a few years of his later life. He died just before turning sixty having spent two thirds of his life as an ordinary English gentleman. A teleological view would point to his cause becoming far from 'disillusioned' given that England was never the same again. England may not have become the Godly nation he strived for, but England was never again governed by the crown in the same way and the concept of rule by 'divine right of kings' ceased to carry weight in the collective English conscience.

Unfortunately not all of Cromwell's actions were quite so chivalrous. It becomes particularly difficult to defend our Lord Protector when attempting to justify the events which took place in Ireland between 5 August 1649 and 26 May 1650. The historian is forced to consider whether Cromwell was truly a man of God, in allowing the atrocities that unfolded at Drogheda and Wexford. According to evidence, some offer of quarter was given to a few Irish soldiers and officers at Drogheda; however, once Cromwell breeched the town defences and seized key buildings, some four thousand combatants and civilians were 'put to the sword'. Parliamentarian forces swept through the streets of Drogheda 'like the black death', slaughtering what futile resistance was left. Priests and Friars took the brunt of Cromwell's rage that day. No one was spared. It is said his hatred for the Catholics and the Irish was at its highest at this point in time:

> Many and terrible were the Irish stories which grew and grew out of the fearful doings of that day and night at Drogheda; there were tales of young virgins killed by soldiers, of Jesuit priests pierced with stakes in the market-place, of children used as shields by the assailants of the church, although Oliver's own mercy was said to have been stirred by the sight of a tiny baby still trying hopelessly to feed from the breast of its dead mother

Although there are valid military reasons for acting as he did, it seems his motives were more sinister at the time. It was out of character, as records tell us Cromwell, as a soldier, always conducted mercy in a compassionate fashion, but Ireland was uncalculated butchery from a man who lost control. Cromwell's infamous reflections were 'I am persuaded that this is a righteous judgement of God upon these barbarous wretches, who have imbrued their hands in so much innocent blood' – the latter referring to Catholics terrorising protestants in Ireland.

Wexford, by many accounts, was a worse atrocity than Drogheda. Where at Drogheda there maybe the excuse of the difficulty in distinguishing between combatants and civilians, at Wexford, one thousand five hundred blatant innocents (women and children) were massacred in the market cross. Today there stands a plaque in Wexford commemorating that terrible day. It is sad that such incidents have blackened Cromwell's name for over three hundred years but in defence of the Lord Protector, counter-arguments are available and objectively must be heard. The rules of war at the time, as far as sieges are concerned, were as such that if the defending commander refuses to surrender, and the town was taken by the offensive force, the commander puts at risk the lives of all those able-bodied who could be construed as combatants. Thereafter, quarter could not be demanded. This rule of no quarter given once defences are breeched was designed to prevent long and bloody battles as garrisons would surrender quickly. Such a rule was still observed up until the Napoleonic Wars, more than a hundred and fifty years later. Such rules of engagement were being established on the back of the atrociously violent and bloody Thirty Years War. Written texts at the time persuaded that to kill prisoners of war was lawful and advocated the slaughter of women and children were permitted to have impunity and understood in the rights of war. By no means excusing the horror of Drogheda and Wexford, we must be mindful that once Cromwell took these towns by force, conventions were that no quarter could have been expected. Quarter was not discussed. Even if it was suggested to him, Cromwell would never have agreed. Orders were given to put to death all those who had borne arms, thus officially sparing civilians, yet many were slaughtered probably in the confusion and chaotic conditions, making it difficult to distinguish between militant and civilian. In defence of Oliver, nowhere in history states that he gave direct orders to massacre civilians. It should also be noted, that in the following years, stories of these incidents grew emphatically fictitious and grossly embellished. The distinguished author, Michael Braddick, in his very comprehensive work *God's Fury, England's Fire*, states that 'English reports of atrocities in Ireland were wildly exaggerated'. A diametrically opposed view of Cromwell's adversaries indicates that he treated Ireland with enlightenment far ahead of his time, establishing free trade between the two countries and allowing equal access to foreign and colonial markets. Cromwell secured representation for Ireland in parliament, Ireland being allocated thirty members; like Scotland, he ensured they both enjoyed free trade off the back of the empire.

It is with thanks to the incompetency of King Charles, that the political, military and religious space was created for Oliver to make the impact he did. The king's actions and behaviour, particularly towards the end of the civil war, made his tough situation untenable. Charles, during the latter stages, had been planning an Irish intervention on a large scale. His negotiations with the Irish and the Pope included the promise of free and public exercise of their religion and possession of churches uninhabited by Protestants. He also promised to 'relieve Roman Catholics of the oath of supremacy and of penal statutes, to open all offices to them, and pardon all offences, civil and criminal, committed since 23 October 1641.

Unfortunately for Charles, a copy of these negotiations were carelessly captured in battle, and later published by the English parliament, consequently his loss of popularity and loyal sovereignty in England took an irrevocable dive. Charles Stuart was charged as having been trusted with power to govern according to the laws of the land, but violated that trust and had chosen to 'erect an unlimited and tyrannical power'. The speaker of the court read the sentence 'that Charles Stuart, for levying war against the present parliament and people therein represented, should be put to death by beheading, as a tyrant, traitor, murderer, and public enemy of the good people of this land'. The king, defiant to the end, refused to acknowledge any authority of the court, declaring 'the king cannot be tried by any superior jurisdiction on earth'.

Despite the sentence being passed, there remained a deep reluctance by members of the House to sign the death warrant. Cromwell, steadfast as always and enraged by their hypocrisy and pending betrayal of the cause, persuaded with clarity and accuracy fifty nine members to sign the warrant. On 30 January 1649, king Charles I was executed - for Cromwell, a righteous judgement, a just retribution upon the idolater and betrayer of the English church and its people. One week after Charles' execution, parliament declared that:

It hath been found by experience, and this house doth declare, that the office of king in this nation, and to have the power thereof in any single person, is unnecessary, burdensome, and dangerous to the liberty, safety and public interest of the people of this nation; and therefore ought to be abolished.

on the 17 and 19 March, the two acts for abolishing the office of monarchs and the House of Lords were historically passed and to hence forth reverberate through English history forever. Thus the first constitution in English history was written, declaring legislative authority should now be bestowed to the Lord Protector and parliament. It is worth illuminating once again, that at this juncture; Oliver Cromwell refused the crown, emphatically claiming the title of king 'weighed', to him, 'no more than a feather'. He never truly justified why he denied the throne, however, we can infer one reason being that he was very aware many senior officers, as well as those of the Godly observers, would all be opposed to him accepting the title. He sincerely felt it would be an offence to the noblest aspects of Protestantism and that he would have disgraced the cause for the 'people of God'. He suspected that all those who followed him from Edgehill to Marston Moor and Naseby would perceive him as nothing more than an opportunist. One can say with absolute certainty however, that his enigmatic hold over the army was so strong that there is little doubt that if he wanted to accept the title, he could easily have done so, dismissing any descent amongst officers. His popularity was so great; any resistance would have been insignificant. Cromwell initially believed that the restoration of the monarchy was essential for the stability of social order.

It has been construed that he was overtly enthusiastic and too cavalierish when negotiating with the king, however, it often seems like Cromwell acted as a one man force – the total personifying or embodying of the revolution itself, as he is overheard shouting at the Leveller leaders:

> I tell you, sir, you have no other way to deal with these men but to break them or they will break you; yea and bring all the guilt of the blood and treasure shed and spent in this kingdom upon your heads and shoulders, and frustrate and make void all that work that...you...have done. To be broken and routed by such a despicable, contemptible generation of men is unthinkable (p269, The Levellers and English Revolution)

The battle of Naseby, despite parliamentarian forces outnumbering the Royalists, hung in the balance and through oscillating fortunes could have swung either way. The parliamentarian New Model army had only recently been formed; with Royalist commanders such as Lord Digby, in mocking fashion, labelling it the 'New Noddle'; mockery which the Royalist elite would come to humbly regret. The battlefield was situated towards the north-western area of Northamptonshire, close to the border of Leicestershire and just south of Market Harborough – coincidentally the most central points in England. The wet conditions on 14 June 1645, did not prevent the Royalists, early morning, from deploying their ranks according to the king's order of battle. They evidently completed assembling their lines before the parliamentarian forces. Prince Rupert took up position on the ridge with his Royal Cavalry. Opposing the Royalists, Ireton took the left flank, Skippon with the parliamentarian infantry in the centre and Cromwell, commander of the Horse, on the right. The Royalists numbered over nine thousand men compared with the parliamentarian force of around fourteen thousand. Rupert's cavalry amounting to four thousand five hundred against Cromwell's six thousand five hundred. Motivation and morale was key, not only to the political campaign, but on the field of battle also. There is evidence that beliefs and concepts were hugely significant in any army, probably for most of the men who filled the ranks. Soldiers marched holding colours that were defended with stoic bravery and national pride, yet there were hugely contrasting messages and symbolism indicating vast differences in what both armies were conceptually fighting for. The challenging battle cries of 'Queen Mary' (an English tribute to Henrietta and the crown) by the Royalists, to the parliamentarian banners with the words inscribed 'God and our strength'. The parliamentarian side emphasised the religious cause and the Royalist side stressed loyalty to the crown. Michael Braddick indeed mentions that 'the army (parliamentarian) was full of hot protestant teaching, and it seemed clear that it bolstered morale'.

Several testimonies suggest that Cromwell was high in confidence that day, instilled with exultation from the thought of impending battle, feeling exonerated and blessed by the heavenly father. Actual observers, eye witness accounts, recorded Cromwell as having a 'wild glee' on his face, breaking out intermittently with 'exuberant laughter'. For Cromwell, he was immune, impervious in his cause. Ultimately, it proved true. Cromwell laughing to himself, moments before confrontation on the battlefield of Naseby, proves the extent of his trust and faith in the Lord more than any of his previous speeches. Oliver didn't just talk the Gospel, he acted upon it. The battle did not go all of parliaments way though. Ireton, on the left, in spite of outnumbering Rupert's regiments three to two, lost contact with his own men, was wounded by a pike and taken prisoner. The opening inspiring charge led by Prince Rupert was totally successful. Even the outnumbered Royalist infantry were making gains in the centre against Skippon, however, Fairfax's men stood firm as always. On the right, it was a very different story. Cromwell, his laughter turned to a deep meditative silence and imbued with Godly conviction, drew up his ranks in three battle lines, at the helm his own loyal veterans of the Eastern Association and joined at the back by the Lincolnshire Horse of Rossiter. It was at Naseby, that Cromwell proved to be the master tactician over Rupert. Oliver led a thunderous charge into Langdale who consequently routed off the field. As one regiment followed the rout, passing the close-by king (who momentarily considered counter-charging Cromwell himself only to be held back by his entourage), Cromwell regrouped the other two regiments and clattered into the Royalist flank like 'the mighty iron hammer hurled by Thor'. Rupert, having won his initial charge the other side of the field, wasted time plundering the parliamentarian baggage train, only to find upon his return, the battle as good as lost. Cromwell's Ironsides, even in the presence of complete victory, held their discipline and did not pursue enemy wagons in search of lustful desires.

Two monuments are erect in the area, one obelisk commemorating the field as hosting 'the great and decisive battle'. Although a smaller fight than Marston Moor, and less casualties, Naseby was the most decisive confrontation of the entire conflict. We know Fairfax lost around two hundred and fifty men and the king a thousand but completely lost his infantry, some four thousand taken prisoner and two thousand horse. On the 19 June, a thanksgiving day was established to commemorate the victory.

Cromwell's foreign policy could justifiably be described as advanced, having transformed England's fragile position in to a rising superpower, an imperial force to be reckoned with. Attention turned to Spain after the dust settled at home, Spain being the 'champions of Catholicism' at the time, though not the reason for hostilities, certainly aided the cause. The project was to attack and possess Spanish assets in the West Indies and transform them into colonies. Spain, although angered, was reluctant to allow a full escalation of war. In contrast, Cromwell was very much in favour of a conflict with 'the Spaniards'. He subsequently gave the Spanish ambassador ultimatums which could not have possibly been contemplated in all seriousness by the king of Spain. It was under Cromwell's protectorate that England saw the dawn of its great navy, a nation beginning to realise its true potential. A navy which would go on to dominate the world for the next three hundred years. This conscious use of superior sea power became instrumental in the acquisition of Jamaica and Barbados. There a reported furious reaction by the Spanish throne, yet their council was still very much against the idea of an Anglo-Spanish war. 'Old Oliver' continued to provoke, bolstered by the very favourable turn of events in England's new position under the Lord Protector. In this regard, assurance was gained from the successful and significant possession of the strategically important island of Gibraltar. Access to the Mediterranean and the West Indies was now wide open and secured. In 1653, he also instigated negotiations for an Anglo-Portuguese commercial alliance. During this period, Cromwell developed relations with the Bays in Morocco and Tunis enabling greater access for trade. The Venetian Ambassador was said to have remarked on 'his unpretending manner of life, remote from all display and pomp'.

The war with Spain was met with success after success, the most important coming in 1656 where a Spanish treasure fleet returning from South America was entirely destroyed, the coffers of Spain losing some six hundred thousand pieces. The following year, Cromwell's great Admiral Blake, with a characteristically swift and brave attack, wiped out the Spaniards at the port of Santa Cruz. Never once did Cromwell seek praise, gratitude or thanks but only ever maintained 'there is not rejoicing simply in a low or high estate, in riches or poverty, but only in the Lord'. He believed feverishly that on the day of judgement, men will be asked not if they believed, but if they acted. Explaining the world can be carried out by Catholic priests, but the puritans drive was to change it by right action. It was some of his great victories over Spain that generated an enthusiasm as to inspire such songs:

Our Lord Protector looking with disdain,
Upon this guided majesty of Spain,

Our actions solid virtue did oppose,
To the rich troublers of the world's repose

There is no doubting that colonial expansion, free trade from governmental interference, parliamentary elected governance, the National Union, agricultural capitalism and religious toleration all came about and flourished under Oliver Cromwell. He is the father of the restoration of the British Empire, restoring international respect, envy, competitiveness and fear. The growing greatness of Britain by the development of his policies and considerations were precisely what enabled Britain to become powerful in the coming centuries. The lasting consequences of the revolution, with reinvigorated English patriotism inextricably fused with religion and liberty and the rise of the middle class, marks a point in history where one man taught the English Lions to roar once more. Only this time, the whole world would feel its aftershocks. Oliver's formation of a new popular national conscience took England to the brink of glory. The writer Edward Hyde, wrote 'Cromwell's greatness at home was but a shadow of the glory he had abroad'. William Godwin claimed 'the government of England had never been so completely freed from the fear of all enemies, both from within and without' as in the period of Oliver Cromwell.

The amount of proclamations, poems and references to Cromwell are endless, but testify to the impact on our national conscience his legacy has left. One of the most famous, written by another national treasure, John Milton, declared 'Cromwell, our chief of men, who though a cloud not of war only, but detractions rude, guided by faith and matchless fortitude, to peace and truth thy glorious way hast ploughed. This an example of how contemporary minds reflected upon Oliver Cromwell. When putting the case forward, that he is one of England's greats, it is difficult to compete with expressions composed by that of John Milton, William Godwin, Frances Bacon and the like. Words cannot do justice to such a rare leader. He was not an ambitious man, attempting to climb his way to the top, but rather a working man called to his duty in service of his country. His unique quality was his ability to understand and live, work, fight and walk with his fellow Englishmen; a founding quality which bound the army's loyalty to him forever. In not dismissing his vengeful side, the source of a rage which thrust him into battle with complete disregard for his own life, rage which compelled him to slaughter catholic priests and behead his king. Lest we forget his sincere and true love for England itself. His love of all things English, the countryside, the weather, his love for animals particularly dogs and horses, all spiritually united him with the very people he served most – the common man. Antonia Fraser emotionally summarises what our one Lord Protector represents then and now:

> To the soldier a source of inspiration, to the revolutionary a source of magic confidence…more powerfully and in his later years, he speaks to us of hope, such men can and will exist. And with them comes vigilance for the morality of government, belief in the light of leadership.

What would Cromwell think of us now? Perhaps an idolatrous, lazy, delinquent, profane, ignorant and hypocritical generation void of principles long buried with our ancestors. Perhaps he would have cause for concern, but whatever we think of Cromwell, the liberty and freedoms we so naively enjoy today, are humbly indebted to our once Lord Protector of the realm. The guiding axiom of his life was to serve ordinary men, to secure their civil liberties as citizens and spiritual liberties as Christians. It was for us he fought against the highest order, to take down the most corrupt king ever to grace the English throne and the equally contaminated ecclesiastical system. To Oliver Cromwell, the essence of puritanism was to lead a good and honest life and he longed to see the time when 'it would be shameful to see men bold in sin and profaneness'. Such a noble cause that often the attempt to interpret such ideals into the desert of the real disappointingly fails. With his grievous dismay, he did not manage (practically or ideologically) to make England puritan. He did, however, bequeath a transcendent loyalty from the army and the common man, to rival only that of Henry V. His position of one of England's Three Lions and one of the greatest Englishmen of all time is justifiably assured.

Timeline of Oliver Cromwell

1599 –   25 April Born at Huntingdon.

1616 –   Cromwell attends Sidney Sussex College, Cambridge.

1617 –   June – Death of Robert Cromwell, Oliver Cromwell's father.

Leaves Cambridge to return home.

1620   22 August – Marries Elizabeth Bourchier in London.

1621 –   Birth of his son Robert.

1623 –   Birth of his son Oliver.

1624 –   Birth of his daughter Bridget.

1625 –   Death of King James I. Accession of King Charles I.

1626 –   Birth of his son Richard.

1628 –   Birth of his son Henry.

March – MP in the House of Commons for Huntingdon.

1629   March – Dissolution of Parliament by King Charles I

Cromwell returns to East Anglia.

Birth of his daughter Elizabeth.

1636 –   Moves to Ely.

1637 –   Birth of his daughter Mary.

1638 –   First of the Bishops War.

Birth of his daughter Frances.

1639 –   Death of his son Robert.

1640 –   Short Parliament. MP for Cambridge.

1641   October – Irish Massacres.

1642   January – The King attempts to arrest five Members of Parliament but fails.

The King leaves London.

22 August – Charles raises the standard at Nottingham.

23 October – Battle of Edgehill.

1643   February – Cromwell made Colonel in the Eastern Association.

13 May – Battle of Grantham.

28 July – Battle of Gainsborough.

10 October – Battle of Winceby.

1644 –   Cromwell made Lieutenant-General.

Death of his son Oliver.

2 July – Battle of Marston Moor.

27 October – Second battle of Newbury.

9 December – Proposal of Self-Denying Ordinance.

1645   14 June – Battle of Naseby.

1646   27 April – King escapes the Scots at Newark.

24 June – Surrender of Oxford.

1647	3 June – Charles captured at Holdenby House.
	Cromwell leaves London for the Army.
	6 August – Army marches through London.
	11 November – The King flees to Carisbrooke Castle, Isle of Wight.
1648	30 April – Start of Second Civil War.
	17 August – Battle of Preston.
	October – Cromwell besieges Pontefract Castle.
1649	20 January – Trial of King Charles I opened.
	30 January – King Charles executed.
	15 August – Arrives in Ireland.
	11 September – Battle of Drogheda.
	October – Siege of Wexford.
1650	April – Siege of Clonmell.
	26 May – Leaves Ireland to head home.
1653	16 December – Cromwell becomes Lord Protector of England and the Colonies.
1654	September – Cromwell's coaching accident.
	Death of his mother.
	December – Begins expedition to the West Indies.
1655	22 January – Cromwell dissolves First Protectorate Parliament.
	May – Conquest of Jamaica.
1656 –	Second Protectorate Parliament.

1657   April – Cromwell is offered Kingship of England.

         8 May – Rejects offer.

         26 June – Becomes Lord Protector.

1658 –   Death of his daughter Elizabeth Claypole.

         3 September – Death of Oliver Cromwell.

CHAPTER 5

Winston Churchill:
War Leader

Hitler knows that he will have to break us in this
island or lose the war. If we can stand up to him
all Europe may be free and the life of the world
may move forward into broad, sunlit uplands.
But if we fail, then the whole world, including
the United States...will sink into the abyss of a
new Dark Age...let us therefore brace ourselves
to our duties and so bear ourselves that if the
British Empire and its Commonwealth last for a
thousand years, men will still say '*this* was their
finest hour'

(June 1940)

And so we arrive at our most recent and dearly departed
lion, whose echoing roar rallied a nation on the brink
of defeat, who defined a people's will to victory as
'unbreakable': Winston Churchill. It is perhaps more app-
ropriate to begin this chapter by observing Churchill's
end rather than his beginning. After three previous
strokes, on 10 January, 1965, a fourth devastating stroke

descended upon him resulting in his passing two weeks later at the age of 90. His death marked a heroic moment for Great Britain as his life embodied the spirit of a nation, a nation which recognised, with overwhelming pride and love, the passing of one of its own, one of their greatest fellow countrymen to have ever lived. All his domestic political discrepancies side-lined and his incongruent character traits accepted. Britain was simply worse without him. It was unanimously agreed to bury Churchill with all the splendour and symbolism of a distinguished warrior. Over three hundred thousand mourners were present as his coffin was escorted to Westminster Hall. With the honour of a state funeral at St Paul's Cathedral, it was graced with the presence of the Queen, who traditionally only attends the funerals of other royal members by protocol. Before sailing up the river Thames to Waterloo station, his coffin was joined by the Royal Scots Fusiliers and Grenadier Guardsmen who he fought side by side with in France 1915. Cadets from Sandhurst were also present, reminding the nation of the origins of his distinguished military career many decades earlier. It marked the first state funeral for a commoner since the Duke of Wellington in 1852. Churchill is perhaps considered as the greatest leader in war this country has ever known; not because he was a superior strategist like Cromwell or a seasoned warrior like Henry the V, but because he stood as an impervious beacon for his country's will to win, a steadfast voice in the darkness which encapsulated the very essence of what it is to be British under the threat of war.

The only Prime minister also to undertake simultaneously the role of Minister of Defence, the effect he had on the fighting men and women of the British Isles was profound. The way he flung himself into the cause head first was unique. He once referred to himself as 'merely the lion's roar' inferring the beating heart was the people of Britain. The connection to his nation is an overwhelmingly emotional one, deeply fatalistic over his intertwined destiny with Britain, his unwavering courage in the blackest hours came from his deep 'bulldog' conviction that Britain could not lose. Lord Attlee once said he had the nerves of a rhinoceros. Churchill himself emphatically claimed with his typical charisma 'I know I can save this country, and I know that nobody else can'. Despite other sides to his reputation, he was resolute and fearless, dedicated to the armed forces and reliable and dependable in meeting adversity without faltering. His predilection for what he called 'feat of arms' was tireless and never-ending. He continuously wanted the forces to hammer away at the enemy, day and night, on all fronts, often irritated when things were quiet. Action, not politics was truly what he understood. In the midst of the sudden realisation of the dramatic conduct of the war, there was a general sense that this unlikely hero was head and shoulders above any of his contemporaries. Maybe the author John Keegan is right; that he 'could seem a figure of exaggerated stature' and 'seemed anything but heroic' with his 'shapeless siren suit, comic stove pipe hat and signatory cigar wedged between flabby fingers', appearing 'wholly unsoldierly'. Yet this seems only to add to his appeal as a leader of the people, rough and ready void of any sartorial elegance, pomp or lavish circumstance. While often very outspoken about the colonies, the empire and the commonwealth, he was far more reserved about Britain, holding her closely to his chest. England, its glory and all it stood for was the limit of his passion. Passion for Churchill has no limit amongst the people of England.

Winston Leonard Spencer Churchill graced the world on the morning of 30 November 1874 at Blenheim Palace, a large courtly house belonging to the Marlborough family. The name Winston was given to him in remembrance of one of his ancestors, Sir Winston Churchill of 1620 to 1688, a relative who is recognised as establishing the family credentials. There are some similarities between the two men, the first Sir Winston was a soldier, and served in the English Civil War on the Royalist side which cost him his family fortune after the Parliamentarians eventually emerged victorious. The name Leonard was taken from Lady Randolph's father Leonard Jerome, a very successful businessman from New York. In his memoirs – *My Early Life,* he recollects his distant relationship with his parents, who always seemed to be away on official engagements. Consequently, he talks warmly of his nanny, Mrs Elizabeth Everest. Until the age of six, he remembers having only a handful of conversations with his parents, and to compound this relationship, in 1881, at the tender age of seven, he was sent to preparatory school in Ascot. Around this period Churchill describes himself as being 'troublesome' and his attendance here lasted only for two years. He was then educated in Brighton in a more relaxed and less academically intense environment where young Winston settled down. After a three year period, he attended one of the most considerably ranked public schools in England – Harrow. It was here by his own confession, he struggled with the Classics and Maths but English and History were interesting subjects to him and he consequently performed well in these.

After a year at Harrow, he was transferred to the Army Class which was specifically geared towards preparation for joining the Royal Military Academy at Sandhurst. As a child, Winston had an extensive collection of toy soldiers, spending hours with them in solitude, and with the backing of his father for the Military Academy, Winston felt very much at home. It did, however, take him three attempts at taking the entrance exam to pass for Sandhurst, largely because of his Maths. His score led him to be offered a cavalry cadetship, not quite enough to make infantry. This was largely due to the fact that the infantry was more popular with applicants because members of the cavalry regiment had to buy and maintain their own horses – a relatively expensive occupational necessity. Churchill enjoyed his time at Sandhurst, particularly the practical hands on side of things. Here he found guidance, discipline and learnt the art of war and military strategy from the masters. This was enriched by his own passionate reading of English Literature and history, acquainting himself with the likes of Thomas Macaulay, Henry Hallam and Rudyard Kipling – all members of that great traditional British flock that advocated the greatness of the empire and enforced imperial discourse during their authorship. Later, his passions and influences became evident in his speeches; through literature and rhetoric he echoed the grand narratives of the fading greatness of the British Empire:

Once again the British Commonwealth and Empire emerges safe, undiminished and united from a mortal struggle. Monstrous tyrannies which menaced our life have been beaten to the ground in ruin, and a brighter radiance illumines the Imperial Crown...Brighter because it comes not only from the fierce but fading glow of military achievements but because there mingle with it in mellow splendour the hope, joys and blessings of mankind. This is the true glory, and long will it gleam on our forward path.

In December 1894, he graduated Sandhurst finishing a very respectable eighth out of 150, revealing at an early stage his distinguished military capabilities. Upon his exit from Sandhurst he was commissioned as a subaltern, the lowest ranked officer, in the 4th Queen's Hussars. During the same period, on 24th January 1895, Churchill's father Lord Randolph passed away at age 45. It was this, in part, which exacerbated Winston's belief that Churchills die young. Ironically, despite the alcohol, cigars and an unbalanced diet, he reached the grand age of ninety, but the intensity to complete all his quests and servitude (as though running out of time) remained with him until the end.

In the summer of 1895 Churchill moved to the Military barracks in Aldershot. It was here where he became a renowned Polo player, representing the regiment in many tournaments. During his two and a half months leave, while most of his fellow officers went off visiting family, Churchill decided he wanted combat experience and constructively entered the war zone of the Spanish campaign in Cuba. A London newspaper, *The Daily Graphic,* commissioned him to write up his observations and to document and report back intelligence. In many ways, this was the beginning of his interest and enthusiasm for espionage and gathering intel. Churchill spent his 21st birthday on the island and experienced for the first time what it was like to be shot at in a live war situation, much to his enthusiasm. Churchill was generally an avid writer and reader and in his memoirs, *My Early Life*, he often recollects his earliest memories with a sense of longing and nostalgia. The example below reflects his thoughts on England in the context of originating from aristocratic circles, England in the broadest sense described as now having lost a sense of community and cohesion:

> In those days English society still existed in its old form. It was a brilliant and powerful thing, with standards of conduct and methods of enforcing them now altogether forgotten. In a very large degree every one knew every one else and who they were. The few hundred great families who had governed England for so many generations and had seen her rise to the greatness of her glory, were interrelated to an enormous extent by marriage. Everywhere one met friends and kinsfolk

This passage, fraught with imperial and colonial discourse, abruptly reminds us of his membership of the ruling class, whose philosophical outlook is firmly anchored in the superiority of the English gentlemen and the enlightenment the British Empire brought to the world.

In September 1896, he was commissioned to join the Malakand Field Force in the North West Frontier (near the Afghan border) and write regular reviews on the campaign for the *Telegraph*. In these writings he described how he attempted to rescue a fallen officer but was challenged and forced back by the Pathans and helplessly watched the onslaught as they cut the man to pieces before Churchill's eyes. Churchill was restrained by his comrades, but his bravery and careless disregard for his own safety became apparent as a young officer. During this particular campaign Churchill recollects coming under fire fifteen times, but, by his own admission, took unnecessary risks in retrospect. This episode enabled him to finish *The Story of the Malakand Field Force* which was published in 1898. While writing his next work, *Savrola* (published a few years later in 1900), Churchill became attached to the 21st Lancers in Egypt while simultaneously writing articles for the *Morning Post* at £15 a column. By September 1898 he was making his way up the Nile to rendezvous with Kitchener's army, not far from Khartoum, where the battle of Omdurman would take place on the 2 September. As the Dervish forces were pushed back, Churchill's cavalry brigade, some 300 Lancers, were ordered to secure a path through the retreating army. While pursuing this objective, they attacked a small group of around 150 Dervish infantry, who, armed apparently only with spears, were in between the British forces and the main Dervish force. As Churchill's unit advanced they came under heavy rifle fire and were confronted by more than 2000 Dervishes who were concealed behind the others. His Lancers committed to full charge and slammed the middle of the Dervish ranks heavily outnumbered. Churchill was knocked clean off his horse and literally fought for his life:

> I had the impression of scattered Dervishes running to and fro in all directions. Straight

before me a man threw himself on the ground...I saw the gleam of his curved sword as he drew it back...I had room and time enough to turn my pony out of his reach, and leaning over the off side I fired two shots into him at about three yards. As I straightened myself into the saddle, I saw before me another figure with uplifted sword. I raised my pistol and fired. So close were we that the pistol itself actually struck him.

The bulldog wanted to mount a second charge after the retreating Dervishes, jumping back on his horse and smelling victory, however, after losing five officers and sixty-five men, concluded one of the last cavalry charges of its kind by the British Army. Three Victoria Crosses were awarded for this extraordinary engagement. Churchill remarkably found himself completely unharmed. Winston, having faithfully documented everything and using his written reports, published *The River War* in 1899, covering his account of the Sudan campaign.

By 1899, Churchill became involved in the Boer War as a soldier and was taken prisoner after an armoured train transporting British personnel came under heavy artillery and rifle-fire, derailing several carriages. After helping wounded soldiers back on to one of the engines, heading back for the others he encountered two Boer soldiers. In attempting to escape from them, he ran into another Boer, mounted and pointing his rifle at Churchill. He was then taken to Pretoria with the other prisoners until he pulled off a daring escape by climbing over the prison wall on the evening of 12 December. Wandering around in Pretoria was perhaps more dangerous than behind prison walls and in making it to the outskirts of the city, he managed to climb aboard a commercial train. The Boers sent out a warrant of his arrest, with a fairly accurate description of Churchill – 'Englishman 25 years old, about 5ft 8iches, average build, walks with a slight stoop, pale appearance, red brown hair, almost invisible small moustache, speaks through the nose, cannot pronounce the letter "s", cannot speak Dutch'. Upon reaching a state of desperation, Churchill decided to approach a house, fortunately belonging to a John Howard, a British mine manager who helped facilitate Churchill's eventual return home. When news of his escape hit the press, his fame reached heroic proportions amidst a very difficult period for Britain concerning the Boer War. Rather than return straight to England, he requested his commissioning into the South African Light Horse, a less committing regiment which allowed him more time to focus on his report writing. While in South Africa, he managed to write two further books – *London to Ladysmith via Pretoria* and *Ian Hamilton's March* which were published in 1900. This point marks the closure of his active duty as a fighting soldier, as he returned to focus his boundless energy on his astonishing political career.

He first took his seat in the House of Commons on February 14, 1901 as a Conservative member of parliament. At the time, the Tories and Liberals were vying for power. The Conservative position gained the upper hand as it expressed patriotic enthusiasm for the Boar war, sentiments which were popular at the time. Liberal's anti-war policies did them no favours. This played into Churchill's hands, although it can be argued he was not a whole-hearted conservative, though shared many tory values. His military knowledge was extensive and made him question the logic of British efforts to emulate Germany and France in expanding the army. He was suspicious and did not understand the secretary of state for war, John Brodwick, who was introducing plans to increase military spending. Public funds would be put in the development of three army corps, much to Churchill's bemusement, as he put it 'one was quite enough to fight savages and three not enough even to begin to fight Europeans'. Germany, which had the largest army in Europe, had already started developing a more sophisticated navy and more than twenty army corps uniformed and ready. In Churchill's view, this three corps investment made no sense, was neither here nor there, and drawing on his own recent war experiences involving modern, complex weapons in Sudan and South Africa, he gave a stark warning that 'a European war cannot be anything other than a cruel, heartrending struggle, which, if we are ever to enjoy the fruits of victory, must demand, perhaps for several years, the whole manhood of the nation'.

With such a blunt opposition to some conservative policies like this, he was perceived as a Tory radical and began to associate with members of the Liberal opposition; one in particular – David Lloyd George. They had some fundamental shared concerns including the generosity to the defeated Boers, the maintenance of free trade and reduced military spending. On May 31, 1904, he entered the House of Commons and 'crossed the floor' to sit with the Liberals. Instead of turning left to sit with the Conservatives, he turned right to sit with the Liberal opposition; an act of betrayal to many core Conservative members who accused him of selfish political manoeuvring and serving only self-interest. Although forthcoming over his ambition to be Prime Minister, he pursued policies that he thought benefitted the working man; greater educational opportunities, better health care, shorter working hours, old-age pensions and an early form of job seekers allowance. Such ideas at the time were socially revolutionary and David Lloyd George took most of the acclaim for the success of these policies. Churchill himself, however, is closely attributed to the establishment of one bill - a minimum wage for groups of low paid workers who consisted of mostly women workers in exploited situations. Both Lloyd George and Churchill set in motion the foundations of the modern Welfare State.

In October, 1911, he was appointed as First Lord of the Admiralty where he quickly introduced plans to modernise and update the Navy by converting the Naval Air Service into a fighting force and not simply for reconnaissance. In addition he wanted the fleet to be driven by the new oil-burning engines as opposed to the coal-burning engines and set about creating a separate Naval War Staff. Churchill's aim was simple. After previous diplomatic incidents with Germany escalating nearly to the point of conflict, he wanted the fleet to be ready and prepared for an eruption of war, by which he was utterly convinced, would happen within a few years at the most. In 1914, war did come. As the Austro-Hungarian army invaded Serbia, Russia and subsequently France joined the fight in favour of Serbia due to their personal treaty obligations, as did Germany in support of the Austro-Hungarian Empire. Churchill put the British Navy on alert and deployed a battle fleet near the Orkneys where strategically it could defend the

North Sea. On 3 August, Germany declared war on France and Belgium, but Britain's participation was still not guaranteed nor committed. At a cabinet meeting it was agreed to give Germany an ultimatum: to stop its advance on Belgium (Germany's first strategic priority) or face war with Britain. On 4 August, with no response, Germany and Britain were now at war, a war in which Churchill became very involved in the daily operations of the navy, making strategic decisions and issuing orders. He also directed what was called the 'Dunkirk Circus', sending three squadrons of bombers from the Naval Air Service to Northern France to bomb the German advance. In July, 1916, the Allied forces began their offense on the Somme which included some 19000 British fatalities, in addition to around 57000 casualties - the largest suffered by any British army in a single day. Right up to the end of autumn, the French and British forces had advanced just five miles.

The Bolshevik Revolution in Russia and the Americans joining the war in 1917 had a large impact on the war. Towards the end of 1918 the Ottoman and Austro-Hungarian Empires signed an armistice with the Allied forces, leaving Germany isolated. Allied victory came shortly in the following year. Churchill recollects the chiming of Big Ben at the hour of eleven from a hotel room in Westminster. He also recalls the wild and emotional celebrations in the immediate aftermath, with chaotic streams of people pouring out of buildings and into the streets of London.

Between the two great wars of the twentieth century, Ireland dominated English politics and became one of the most difficult situations for Churchill to confront in all his political life. The border juxtaposed by the catholic majority and protestant minority in Ireland became the bane of the British Empire itself. The First World War had merely postponed the conflict by a mutual agreement with all those involved, to set aside differences until the outcome of the war was resolved. The refusal of the Protestants to accept Home Rule by the Catholics sparked an intense political crisis during this period. The Easter Rising in 1916 was met with such force that its severity provoked outrage amongst even the moderate Irish. The brutal tactics adopted by the British led to an all-out insurrection for Churchill to handle. He commissioned the creation of the military anti-terror units of the Black and Tans and the 'Auxies' who adopted similar tactics to the IRA. With relentless and unceasing Catholic support, Churchill conceded the partition of Ireland into a small Protestant North and larger Catholic South. In October, 1921, he conducted a meeting with the two prominent Irish leaders – Arthur Griffith (a moderate idealist) and Michael Collins (an Irish militant). Churchill being a fighting man at heart immediately engaged with Michael Collins and the pair developed a very positive relationship based on mutual respect and reluctant admiration. One contemporary noted that they 'appear to fascinate each other and are bosom friends'. Collins, often referred to as 'the Big Fellow', eventually agreed a compromise leading to the creation of an Irish Free State still within the British Empire. After signing the treaty he famously stated 'I may have signed my death warrant'. IRA purists consequently refused the agreement leading to a civil war. Michael Collins was murdered in an anti-Free State ambush in 1922 – his last words were reported to have been 'Tell Winston we could never have done it without him'. It was the courage and character of Michael Collins that changed Winston's attitude towards the Irish in general, as he came to sincerely admire and respect the IRA guerrilla leader. His Unionist disposition was shaken, and the big Irishman always remained close to Churchill's heart. So effective was Sinn Fein's tactics that, in 1940, in the event of a German invasion, Churchill instructed the head of Special Operations to adopt a similar type of guerrilla warfare, rendering any invading campaign by the Germans virtually impossible to sustain.

Palestine also became an issue, to which Churchill was to be central in 1921. Palestine, which had been a province of the Ottoman Empire for a lengthy period of time, was handed over to Britain by mandate of the League of Nations at the end of the First World War. Though historically the homeland of the Jewish people, it was inhabited by an overwhelming Arab majority. In 1917, the Jews were promised a return to their homeland by the British government, and Churchill as the Colonial Secretary, in 1921, became the administrator of the Balfour Declaration. He declared in the House of Commons, however, that 'the rights of the existing non-Jewish population would be strictly preserved'. In light of the proceeding events, one must question the sincerity of his words on this occasion. The rights of the Muslim population were not respected and today this conflict has so much to answer for the state of interplay between East and West. There were many events in Churchill's life during the decade after the First World War, however Churchill's glorious and most memorable days were still to come. Administering the Balfour Declaration related to Palestine was certainly not his finest hour.

Some fourteen years after the atrocities of the First World War, a new hate was stirring in Germany, with a growing fascist ideology and violent ambitions. The unrealistic and excessively harsh stipulations of the Treaty of Versailles was partly to blame for the flourishing of the Nazi party, demanding vast repayments and compensation for the previous war, leading to an unemployment epidemic and wide scale depression. The Germans unsurprisingly turned to nationalism and the rise of Adolf Hitler. In January, 1933, Hitler became Chancellor of Germany and began the insidious reversal of Germany's previous military humiliation by becoming the world's greatest military power. In 1919, the Versailles Treaty denied Germany the luxury of naval forces, air capabilities and deprived it of tanks and artillery. Between 1934 and 1935, Hitler set about building an enormous tank fleet and the Luftwaffe and Britain astonishingly agreed to an amendment of the Versailles Treaty which would allow Germany to construct and deploy submarines. Perhaps the most significant step in rearmament was in 1935 - to reinstate conscription. In just a few years the German army went from being merely symbolic and grossly inferior to its neighbours, to vastly exceeding their strength and capabilities. In the month of June, 1930, during the infamous 'Night of the Long Knives', Hitler had dissenting members of his own Nazi party murdered to facilitate his personal total control. In August, after the death of Hindenburg, he became Head of State, crowning himself 'Fuhrer' and apprehending supreme control of the German armed forces. Hitler's political and ideological tendencies were widely available long before he put them to action in his book *Mein Kampf*

(*My Struggle*), written back in 1924 while in prison. Throughout the 1930's Churchill issued numerous warnings of the growing menace of Nazi Germany, but still Europe did nothing, took no measures and seemed possessed with procrastination watching idly as Germany grew stronger.

In 1934, the German army was outnumbered by the British, even more so by the French and vastly inferior to the Soviet Union's forces. Within three years the balance of power turned upside down. Towards the end of 1938, the German army boasted a numerical strength of forty-six infantry divisions, five Panzer tank divisions and some six-hundred thousand personnel. The Luftwaffe possessed three thousand combat aircraft, which at this stage already outnumbered the Royal Air Force and the Armee de L'Air combined. The French army was large but poorly equipped and the British forces numbering only six infantry divisions and one tank division with two-hundred thousand soldiers, mostly dispersed across the colonies. In November, 1936, Churchill made a critical and damning speech in the House of Commons concerning the lack of effort from the government in prioritising rearmament, which consequently gave Germany more than a two year head start:

I have been staggered by the failure of the House of Commons to react effectively against those dangers [presented by the German rearmament]. That, I am bound to say, I never expected. I never would have believed that we should have been allowed to go on getting into this plight, month by month, year by year...I say that unless the House resolves to find out the truth for itself it

will have committed an act of abdication of duty
without parallel in its long history.

Since 1932, Churchill had been expressing anxieties
about Britain's flippant trivialisation of what was
happening in Germany. As the British and French governments were enforcing a reduced spending plan on
defence, Winston warned 'Not to have an adequate air
force...is to compromise the foundations of national
freedom and independence'. Many in Britain's political
class shrank away at the thought of another grim
confrontation and were subsequently cocooned in a state
of denial, particularly during the early years of Hitler's
Germany. Chamberlain was categorically and naïvely in
denial until the point where his bubble of passivity and
appeasement burst. A handful of ministers, loyal to the
ministerial code and led by Churchill, began to resist
against this collective delusion and reignited Britain's
defensive instincts. In March, 1936, Hitler's forces
entered the demilitarised zone of the Rhineland further
transgressing the Versailles Treaty. This was met with
weak retaliation from Britain and France allowing the
Germans to march through unopposed.

One may ask the question as to why Churchill didn't
supersede Chamberlain at a much earlier stage. It has
been suggested that Churchill was considered to be a
liability, being slightly volatile and perhaps too eager for
confrontation, as opposed to Chamberlain who many
favoured his strategy of diplomacy and attempted
placating of Hitler. Churchill and others were aware,
however, that with such an aggressive totalitarian
disposition, such an approach would ultimately prove
ineffective against Nazi Germany, and worse, send Hitler

a message that Britain would not challenge him unless he directly threatened and contravened British interests. Chamberlain and Daladier (the French Prime Minister) merely encouraged Hitler to do whatever he wanted. As Hitler proceeded to run amuck, Churchill's astuteness enabled him to smell a fight coming a mile away and was chomping at the bit, waiting for his time, waiting to be let off the leash. Little did history know that the British Bulldog would become Britain's most potent and deadly weapon, a raging presence that would nightmarishly haunt Hitler in life and in death. Not through physical strength would triumph come, but through sheer determination, perseverance, tenacity and that legendary 'no surrender – never give up' mentality that corner stoned British mantra throughout the empire.

In March, 1938, the *Anschluss* took place where the German forces marched into Austria with futile resistance and in most cases were disturbingly welcomed. With such considerable support for Hitler (born in Austria himself), Austria overnight became part of the new German Empire, marking the first time Germany had crossed international borders since the First World War. Again, Chamberlain's response was weak, consistent with his policy of appeasement. Attentions were quickly drawn to Czechoslovakia as German forces were quickly gathering along the border near the Sudetenland area, a region heavily populated by Germanic people. The problem was that France had signed a treaty previously with Czechoslovakia guaranteeing their sovereignty. If Germany invaded the Czechs it seemed likely a European war would ensue. Three official meetings took place but at the third, on 29 September, in Munich, attended by Mussolini,

Chamberlain, Hitler and Daladier, all four agreed on the acceptance of a German occupation of Czechoslovakia. Chamberlain upon returning home the next day, feeling rather pleased with himself, held the agreement up and claimed it signified 'peace for our time'. Many MPs shared his view but Churchill could not repress his feelings stating:

> They should know that there has been gross neglect and deficiency in our defences; they should know that we have sustained a defeat without a war, the consequences of which will travel far with us along our road...the whole equilibrium of Europe has been deranged, and the terrible words have been pronounced against the Western democracies: 'Thou art weighed in the balance and found wanting'. And do not suppose that this is the end. This is only the beginning of the reckoning. This is only the first sip ...of a bitter cup which will be proffered to us year by year unless by a supreme recovery of moral health and martial vigour, we arise again and take our stand for freedom as in the old time.

Despite such spine-tingling words, the House of Commons disappointingly took little notice. On 15 March, 1939, German forces occupied Prague and Czechoslovakia was no more. At no time in history had Czechoslovakia ever been a part of German territory, such was the magnitude of this invasion. Hitler, feeling unopposed immediately set his sights on Poland (Germany's neighbouring country to the east) claiming the region known as the 'Polish Corridor' should be annexed to East Prussia. This region included the Polish port of Danzig now called Gdansk. It is at this juncture that Chamberlain finally realised what was going on and guaranteed Poland military intervention if Hitler invaded. In spite of the Nazis being fiercely against the Bolsheviks, Hitler, on 22 August that year signed the Molotov-Ribbentrop Pact with Stalin's Russia secretly dividing territories of central Europe between them while agreeing not to fight each other. Three days later on 25 August, Britain and France formalised a treaty of military intervention concerning Poland, discouraging Hitler's plans to invade Polska which he had organised for the following day. The German attack on Poland began on 31 August. While waiting for the French to make decisions, Chamberlain sent Germany a demand to immediately cease the incursion and withdraw. He sent this at 9 o'clock the next morning, and with no response, Chamberlain announced on national radio two hours later that 'consequently this country is now at war with Germany'. The Russians had grievances with Poland too (for similar reasons that the Versailles Treaty allocated Poland territory that the Soviet Union thought was rightfully theirs). Within just over a year, Germany had overrun Austria, Czechoslovakia and parts of Poland with virtually no physical confrontation. With the Molotov-Ribbentrop Pact negating any threat from the east from Russia, Hitler's confidence was perhaps at its peak.

Throughout the remaining year of 1939 and 1940, while the Russians occupied much of Eastern Europe and attacked Finland, Germany turned to the North and invaded Denmark and Norway. Denmark fell almost straight away but Norway, aided by its harsh mountainous landscape, put up a long resistance with some Anglo-French help. Such was the valour of the Norwegians that Churchill became inspired by their efforts and the Royal Navy won a crushing victory at the battle of Narvik, inflicting heavy damage to the German fleet. The Germans, however, dominated the land campaign and were eventually successful. By May, British and French forces were withdrawing from Trondheim prompting a growing sense of dissatisfaction and criticism in the House of Commons. Chamberlain feeling disoriented, called for his own resignation after a prominent Conservative MP, Leo Amery, told Chamberlain word for word what Oliver Cromwell said to the Long Parliament in 1653 'You have sat too long here for any good you have been doing. Depart, I say, and let us have done with you. In the name of God, go'. On May 10, when King George asked Chamberlain to name his successor (as is tradition), he emphatically claimed it must only be Churchill. The man of the hour stood tall and immediately inherited the dire situation he argued for years to avoid. Churchill was sixty-five, his dream come true, he was ready for action. That month, he made a speech to the House laying down his single objective:

> You ask, what is our policy? I will say, it is to wage war by sea, land and air and with all our might...You ask, what is our aim? I can answer in one word: Victory. Victory at all costs. Victory in spite of all terror. Victory, however long and hard the road may be, for without victory there is no survival.

As Churchill told his War Cabinet he has nothing to offer them but 'blood, toil, tears and sweat', Germany was discreetly pushing through the Ardennes while distractingly occupying allied forces in Belgium. After successfully getting heavily armoured mobile units through the Ardennes, Hitler unleashed the *Blitzkrieg* with superior firepower and surprise. It was a masterful strategy which delivered a heavy payday. Hitler took a dangerous risk though, for if Allied intelligence discovered his forces en route, a large percentage of the German army would have been stranded, cut off and left vulnerable. As it turned out, Hitler practically took France within nine days. It was not the Battle of France, but the Fall of France. The Fuhrer was instantly elevated to God status in Germany, capturing the might of France with such relative ease. General De Gaulle bravely put up some resistance with the surviving French divisions, but the German General Rommel had the better of him wreaking havoc and rampaging all over France. With French units collapsing daily, Belgium capitulating completely, a proposal was put forward by Chamberlain and Halifax in the War Cabinet, for Churchill to consider seeking terms from Hitler. The Lionheart retaliated 'If this long island story of ours is to end at last, let it end only when each one of us lies choking in his own blood upon the ground'. France continuously requested more help from Britain, particularly fighter planes to help their cause, but the circumstances were dire. Churchill and the War Cabinet reluctantly agreed any such help would only further weaken Britain's chances of survival. This, combined with the decision to withdraw at Dunkirk, left a bitterness and resentment between the French and British, France feeling let down by the British lack of help, diametrically opposing British sentiments of disgruntlement at the lack of French resistance in the first place.

Operation Dynamo began on 26 May, the Dunkirk retreat included 333,000 troops who were evacuated and brought back to Britain by 3 June. Around 100,000 were French soldiers. Not only was this probably the lowest point morally for the Allies but militarily they left a huge amount of artillery including tanks and equipment which was badly needed for the continuing effort. France, following an armistice in June, was led by Petain (a veteran of the First World War) who was the head of the Etat Francais with authority over Southern and Central France south of the river Loir. Its new capital of Vichy, offered no resistance to German occupation whatsoever. Petain's refusal to sail the remaining French fleet into British ports (as requested by Churchill) forced the decision by the British to disable the fleet so not to fall into German hands. In July, the French North African ports of Oran and Mers-el-Kabir were attacked killing around 1200 French sailors. This only exacerbated tensions between Britain and what was left of France. Now, standing alone, with the might of the German Empire breathing down our neck, on 4 June, 'good old Winnie' gave the greatest speech of his life, soulful, heart rendering words which reminded us of who we are:

> Even though large parts of Europe and many old and famous States have fallen or may fall into the grip of the Gestapo and all the odious apparatus of Nazi rule, we shall not flag or fail. We shall go on to the end, we shall fight in France, we shall fight on the seas and oceans, we shall fight with growing confidence and growing strength in the air, we shall defend our island, whatever the cost

may be, we shall fight on the beaches, we shall fight on the landing grounds, we shall fight in the fields and in the streets, we shall fight in the hills, we shall never surrender, and even if, which I do not for a moment believe, this island or a large part of it were subjugated and starving, then our Empire beyond the seas, armed and guarded by the British fleet, would carry on the struggle, until, in God's good time, the New World, with all its power and might, steps fourth to the rescue and the liberation of the old.

With no guarantee that the 'New World' would step in, this speech aroused a patriotic war cry across Britain, reminding ourselves that we are a fighting nation, an imperial power like none before or after, forged from two thousand years of proud, stubborn warriors who will not yield before anyone and that Britannia will stare back at her adversaries in raging defiance no matter how great the enemy. Hitler and Germany will fall like all other tyrants before. It was a message that although the French might have given up, the British will not, and whether or not America becomes involved, we would fight 'on, alone if necessary'.

Consistent reconnaissance gathered enough evidence to show that there was a mass build-up of German troops, tanks and equipment concentrating in North-Western France, placing England on red alert through fear of an imminent invasion. Southern and Eastern England particularly shifted into defensive mode. In order for Hitler to give the invasion the green light, he needed to obtain air superiority over the channel. Throughout the month of July German air raids continued with squadrons of fighter planes filling the skies, hunting for Spitfires and attempting to demoralise and subdue the Royal Air Force. Munitions factories and airfields became top priority for German Bombers. Dominating the skies was the only realistic strategy for Hitler if he was serious about invading Britain. If this was not achieved, shipping men and war machines across the channel with the RAF circling above would be extremely risky, particularly bearing in mind the Royal Navy was far stronger than the *Kriegsmarine* (German Navy). This crucial battle of the skies was to become famously known as the battle of Britain. In attempting to suffocate Britain, German U-boats were successful in sinking supply vessels in the Atlantic often leading to short supplies at home. The Luftwaffe pushed harder and harder with night raids of bombing and constant dogfights, always outnumbering the Royal Air Force. The only advantage the RAF had was the fact that they were fighting on top of their own airfields most of the time, on home territory with the ability to refuel quickly and get back in the air. The German planes, however, could only spend around half an hour in British airspace before having to return to Europe to refuel. At one stage, every single squadron Britain had was in the air at the same time. Losses for both sides were desperately high but the British forces edged it by inflicting more German casualties with a ratio of around 2:1 in favour of Britain. Around 15 September saw some of the most intense air battles, with Churchill receiving false alarms that the Germans are crossing the border. With Manchester, Cardiff, Birmingham, Belfast, Coventry, Sheffield and mostly London targeted with high explosives and incendiary bombs, the country suffered large structural damage and thousands of casualties. These bombing raids were later recollected as the *Blitz*. It was a close run contest between the German and British air forces but as the conflict droned on, it was Britain that was winning the war of attrition and for the first time in the war the Germans were starting to lose significantly. Hauntingly similar to Agincourt, the few defeated the many. Churchill himself said 'Never in the field of human conflict has so much been owed by so many to so few'. Churchill was equally touched by the extraordinary resilience and stoicism shown by people who had been hit by German bombs, defying the Germans to keep coming.

With Greece falling to Germany April, 1941, forcing the evacuation of around 50,000 British and Commonwealth soldiers sent to help Greece, in June, Germany ruthlessly and very successfully invaded Russia. With Hitler turning his back on Stalin and the Molotov-Ribbentrop Pact, the Soviet Union was now aligned with the Allied forces. This was good news for Churchill. Winston was categorically anti-Communist till he died and during and after the war only extended his hand of friendship to Stalin in the light of the common enemy of Nazi Germany. Churchill harboured as much hate and loathing of the Soviet system and Stalin as he did for Hitler and Nazi Germany. Hitler and Stalin represented similar ideologies of repression and control. Churchill once said in private in words to the effect that he would drink with the devil himself if it served Britain's cause. In a fight to the death, an ally is an ally in whatever form. As the Allied forces were campaigning in the Mediterranean, the Germans made their way (via Southern Russia) towards the oil fields of the Caucuses.

They were halted by the Red Army at Stalingrad which became the bloodiest battle of the entire war. If Stalingrad (what became Hitler and Stalin's personal battleground) had fallen to the Germans it could have no doubt changed the direction of the war. By February, 1943, Hitler's entire Eastern army was all but destroyed and unserviceable and Germany, arguably never recovered. Stalin, Churchill and Roosevelt met on a number of occasions, notably besides strategy to discuss the future of post war Europe. Although Churchill had generally a good relationship with Roosevelt, it was at these discussions that clear differences emerged over conflicting national aims. Britain was in many ways fighting to defend its empire and the old world in which it enjoyed being a superpower. America's interests lie in creating its own economic and military power in a new world where it was the superpower. It is impossible to deny that America succeeded, in part at Britain's expense, with the exploitation of Britain during the war itself and the post war decolonisation and deconstruction of the British Empire. Churchill was 'Old England' and a true product of imperialism and undoubtedly found this whole process painful. Roosevelt and Stalin met increasingly in private giving Churchill the impression he was left on the bench. The two superpowers of the twentieth century were becoming apparent and Churchill once admitted 'what a small nation we are', comparing Britain to the giants of the United States and the Soviet Union.

In June, 1944, the first D-Day landings hit western France on the beaches known as Utah and Omaha. Although German defences gallantly resisted, the British, American, Canadian and other Allied troops took sections of the German force by total surprise. The Americans took heavy casualties at Omaha beach but managed to secure the sector. Around 3,000 men were killed on the first day. On 12 June, Churchill, aged 69, insisted on attending the beaches a few days after the landing. Some months later he was criticised for the highly controversial commissioning and support of the bombing raid of Dresden. On 14 February, 1945, Allies completely wiped out the centre of Dresden by bombing highly populated areas. The exact number of people killed is unknown but estimates are as high as 30,000 to 40,000. Today, the argument continues as to how justifiable this murderous act was, particularly as the war was almost won. 'Bomber' Harris, who was Head of Bomber Command and close advisor to Churchill, recommended the raid. The desired outcome of wide area bombing was of course to bring the German people to their knees and break their will, but although Nazi Germany committed many war crimes, this remained a morally ambiguous tactical decision. On 12 April, 1945, Roosevelt died of a cerebral haemorrhage. Churchill decided not to go to the funeral, perhaps due to the growing rift between them. On 30 April, Hitler, with the Red Army crashing through the streets of Berlin, committed suicide. The final surrender came on 7 May. Two weeks after Victory Day, Churchill resigned as Prime Minister and set in motion a general election. Stalin's death came in March 1953.

What sustained the British people during the 'stand-alone' period was Churchill's words. Not only did they impress on his people's heart and spirit, but they reached out across the seas to all those who were suffering, appealing to a commonality centring on freedom and humanity which embraced all those against Hitler. They were words filled with hope, love, divine justice and steadfast principles. Hitler spoke rarely after 1939. An aggressive orator, his rhetoric was filled with threats, hatred and condemnation glorifying the denigration of others. In contrast, Churchill in the following broadcast, reached out to the world:

> To all the States or nations bound or free, to all the men in all the lands who care for freedom's cause, to our allies and well-wishers in Europe, to our American friends and helpers drawing ever closer in their might across the ocean: this is the message – Lift up your hearts. All will come right. Out of the depths of sorrow and sacrifice will be born again the glory of mankind.

In many ways, the old British Empire and the England of our imagination, slipped into the chapters of history with Churchill's passing. After a century of global dominance in the modern era, Winston's England bid farewell. Britain has not been the same since, and every day it must renegotiate its identity. It is true that he romanticised the history of his beloved country and in doing so he romanticised its people. Never has such an absence of his figure felt so grave. During the celebrations of VE-Day, he shouted to the crowd 'this is your victory', to which the crowd responded 'no, it's your victory'. Together they had exceeded expectations and Churchill reached a point of total harmonious synchronisation with the identity of his people through war-time Britain. He appealed to England's traditions of greatness. Despite current research exposing all his flaws, his impetuosity, belligerence and political short-comings, his reputation as our greatest war leader lies before us intact and undiminished.

As John Keegan wrote 'The glow of military achievement and the splendour of empire have almost faded away, but a true glory continues to gleam over Churchill's life, works and words'.

Timeline of Winston Churchill

1874 –   November 30 – Born Winston Leonard Spencer-Churchill into an aristocratic family in Oxfordshire, England.

1875-1882 –   Churchill is neglected by his parents and consequently forms a strong bond with his nanny, Mrs. Everest.

1888 –   April 17 – Churchill attends Harrow School where he starts his military career by joining the Harrow Rifle Corps.

1893 –   Churchill attends the Royal Military Academy in Sandhurst and graduates in the top half of his class the next year.

1895 –   January 24 –Churchill's father, Lord Randolph Churchill, dies. Churchill travels to Cuba to observe the Spanish fight Cuban guerrillas and files reports about the conflict.

1896 –   Churchill is assigned to Bombay in British India. He fights against Pashtun tribes and files reports for English newspapers. His reports are compiled and published as Churchill's first book, The Story of the Malakand Field Force.

1898 –   Churchill is transferred to Egypt and takes part in the British re-conquest of Sudan. He participates in one of the last British cavalry charges in history at the Battle of Omdurman.

- A stamp of Churchill as a war correspondent in South Africa, 1899.

1899 –   May 5 –Churchill resigns from the British Army with the intent on starting a political career. Churchill goes by ship to South Africa to report on the Second Boer War. He was captured, but escaped and joined the South African Light Horse.

1900 –   Churchill returns to England and wins a seat in parliament with the Conservative Party.

1904 –   Churchill crosses the floor and joins the Liberal Party.

1905 –   Churchill is promoted to major in the Queen's Own Oxfordshire Hussars. He writes and publishes *Lord Randolph Churchill*, a biography of his father.

1908 –   September 12 – Churchill marries Clementine Hozier with whom he has five children:

Diana (1909-1963), Randolph (1911-1968), Sarah (1914-1982), Marigold (1918-1921) and Mary (1922-).

1909 –   Churchill sets up a Labor Exchanges Act to help unemployed people find work.

1910 –   Churchill is promoted to Home Secretary, responsible for British internal affairs.

1911 –   Churchill becomes First Lord of the Admiralty.

1914 –   Churchill contributes to the salvation of the cities of Calais and Dunkirk from German invasion after the outbreak of World War I.

1915-1916 – Churchill is demoted after the disastrous Gallipoli campaign which left thousands dead in Turkey. Churchill later fights on the Western Front against the Germans.

1923 –   After the war Churchill re-enters politics.

1924 –   Churchill becomes Chancellor of the Exchequer and oversees a calamitous return to the Gold Standard, a system which fixed the price of money to gold and resulted in substantial economic turmoil. Churchill regarded it as the biggest mistake of his life.

1925 –   Churchill re-joins the Conservative Party after holding office as an independent.

1931 –   Churchill speaks out against an Indian independence movement lead by Gandhi.

1931 –   Churchill reaches a low point in his political career, estranged from the Conservative leadership.

1932 –   Churchill speaks out about the dangers of a re-arming and growing Germany.

1939 –   September 3 – Churchill is reappointed First Lord of the Admiralty at the outbreak of World War II.

1940 –   May 10 – British Prime Minister Neville Chamberlain resigns and Churchill becomes Prime Minister.

               - June 18 – Churchill makes his famous "finest hour" speech to the House of Commons. He later creates the Ministry of Defence and puts Lord Beaverbrook in charge of strengthening Britain's air force.

1941 –   August – Churchill meets President Franklin D. Roosevelt for the first time aboard a ship in Newfoundland. The leaders sign the Atlantic Charter, a draft outline for world politics after World War II.

1941 –   December – Churchill suffers a mild heart attack while visiting Roosevelt in the White House.

1943 –   November 28 to December 1 – Churchill, Roosevelt and Soviet leader Joseph Stalin meet at the Tehran Conference.

1944 –   October – Churchill flies to Moscow to meet Stalin and the Soviet leadership. The leaders informally discuss who should have control over what in Europe after the expected fall of Nazi Germany.

1945 –   February 4 - 11 – The Yalta Conference. Churchill meets with the other 'Big Three' leaders, Stalin and Roosevelt, to formally draw up the post-war restructuring of Europe.

-February 13-15 – British and U.S. bombers attack the German city of Dresden, killing up to 30,000 civilians. Some historians claim Churchill was responsible for the attack. - Churchill orders the creation of "Operation Unthinkable", a contingency plan to attack the Soviet Union shortly after the end of the war against Germany.

-May 8 – Churchill announces the German surrender to the British people.

-July 5 – Churchill is defeated in a general election and becomes the Leader of the Opposition.

1946 –   March 5 – Churchill visits the United States, comprehensively defeats President Harry Truman in a game of poker and makes his famous "Iron Curtain" speech about the impending Cold War with the Soviet Union.

1951 –   October 25 – Churchill again becomes Prime Minster.

1953 –   April 23 – Churchill is knighted by Queen Elizabeth II.

June – Churchill suffers a severe stroke at 10 Downing Street.

He retreats to his country home and returns to public life in October.

Churchill receives the Nobel Prize for Literature for his written works, in particular his six-volume The Second World War.

1955 – Churchill retires as Prime Minister and becomes a backbencher.

1956 – February – Churchill suffers another minor stroke.

1964 – Churchill leaves politics.

1965 – January 15 – Churchill suffers another severe stroke.

January 24 – Churchill dies aged 90. He is given a state funeral at London's St Paul's Cathedral.

CHAPTER 6

A Test of England's Fortitude

A nation is not an idea only of local extent and individual momentary aggregation; but it is an idea of continuity, which extends in time ... and in space.

(Ed Burke, 1782)

We have looked at some ideas of what England is, what it once was and some of its greatest advocates. While researching such a rich topic as English identity, a subtle but all important distinction emerges between England the 'state' and the culturally structured elements held close by English people beneath the surface of the 'state': the way we go about our daily business, the local things in life and our everyday work patterns and social habits. These national values can be seen as the true source of a nation's shared character traits residing subliminally beneath the state, where a collective unconscious process can call upon a nation's deepest awareness. Freud saw this as a 'primeval force of extraordinary credulity', and for the social scientist Gustave Le Bon, it constituted the 'psychology of the masses'. Formulated conceptions of the outside world passed on through centuries of English folklore have provided a large contribution to its identity and our collective sense of self. A self-proclaimed national attribute of England - that of continued survival, evidently, has been forged by the contradictory fusion of the formation of an early multicultural society unified by the very threat of 'those cultures from outside' its domain. Reactionists to Anglocentricism are quick to point out the empire did not survive. The response that should be maintained is thus; England is and never was the empire and through all the international power shifts and changes in political and geographical boundaries, England's principle property of survival has endured.

There are elitist assumptions about 'the masses' as being ignorant and dogmatic, and, perhaps there is some truth in this with common folk being by and large blissfully unaware of the grand oligarchic schemes plotted in the political and financial spheres. Nevertheless, the English masses are of a multicultural grain. England as a celebration of multiculturalism can be traced back as far as the Danelaw during the ninth and tenth centuries where the Angles, Danes, Saxons and Norwegians cohabited and eventually coalesced. English ignorance therefore takes on a universal quality, particularly now as our multicultural cohort has swollen immensely over recent times. However opposed to the masses' collective interpretation of identity institutions of power might be, the common representations of the land and its people cannot be ignored. The middle class D.H. Lawrence deeply desired to embrace the common person and their common instincts as he felt middle class England left an identity vacuum which the masses did not suffer from. He expressed a longing to be 'connected to something'. We can infer that 'something' related to the question of identity. With the exception of the leaders included earlier and probably a select few who have not been mentioned such as Queen Victoria or Elizabeth I, Orwell's famous metaphor of our country as 'a family with the wrong members in control' prominently bubbles to the surface. Most of these family members, English politicians filled with nothing but sophistry and illusion, of course don't believe in nationalism. Welsh, Scottish and Irish politicians can employ patriotism in their discourse, but not English statesmen. Not anymore. These so called 'family members' in charge are also responsible for embarrassingly mismanaging social issues such as immigration, education and the welfare state over the last seventy years. The subject of immigration particularly, though peripheral, still remains a relevant factor in the England debate, especially now.

During the late sixties and early seventies, the number of immigrants entering the UK was offset by the amount of emigrants leaving the UK, mostly to Australasia throughout this period. In 1960 and 1961 there was a sudden surge of immigrants from third world countries from the 'New Commonwealth', predominantly from the West Indies and the Indian subcontinent. Yet from 1961 to 1979 emigration exceeded immigration every year. The problem of immigration was not so much the numbers but the fact that an overwhelming majority headed straight for England. It became, in essence, an English problem as during the sixties in Scotland only two out of every thousand had originated in the Commonwealth. This contrasted with an English number six times higher. The seriousness of the immigration problem (exacerbated during the last decade through a severe absence of awareness about who comes in and who goes out) stems from the distinct and appalling lack of exercising control over entry and citizenship. Racial tensions were merely a result of this mismanagement. Peter Clarke in *Hope and Glory* indicates:

> It was the visible presence of 'dark strangers', concentrated in some English towns and cities, which gave immigration statistics a racial edge. The new comers had their own distinctive habits and conventions, from cooking to religion, and, of course, their own distinctive skin colour. English people rarely talked about 'Niggers'- despite the electoral slogan "if you want a nigger for your neighbour, vote labour" – and at the time it was considered polite to avoid speaking of a black population by using the term coloured.

The other issue concerning immigration surrounds the forceful advocacy of a rival code of conduct to that of the home nation. This directly conflicts with England's secular traditional values. Socially, the difficulties dealing with Islamic communities have proven to be a strenuous challenge of integration. Many such communities are resolute in maintaining their own culture to the point of isolating themselves from indigenous communities, a process often perceived in a disrespectful and antagonistic light, invoking anger, frustration and occasional violence. The ugly side of immigration unfortunately manifests itself in ghettoization. In terms of English values, England has and always will welcome visitors both migrant and immigrant. So it should, providing it's for the right reasons. Can nationality be

irreducibly a matter of bloodline or race? No. Is Englishness unique and peculiarly different from its European
neighbours? Absolutely. The point is, that anyone who
lives in England and whole-heartedly adopts English
cultural values will be English regardless of skin colour
or religion. The current reaction to immigration (intensified with the recent green light for Romanians and
Bulgarians to join the party) is manifesting itself in a
growing voice from the right responding to England's
inflating cultural diversity with cries of a broader loss
or erosive sense of English identity.

The question of England's identity raises many social
and cultural issues, neglected issues such as immigration, nationalism and race. The fall of the empire has
not though produced a nation-shattering traumatic
experience socially as many writers proclaim. Foreigners
were far quicker to recognise the changing reality of
Britain's global position than many Britons. Britain
problematically convinced itself of the presupposed
continuity of its imperial ideology into the twentieth
century. At the heart of British imperialism lay the
concept of free trade but the reality was closer to exploitation and expansion anchoring on the supremacy of a
dominant Navy. In many ways the loss of the empire
represents a 'civilised transition to the birth of a healthier
multicultural Commonwealth'. The Commonwealth as
opposed to the Empire connotes a fairer and nobler
relationship between the former colonised and the
coloniser, with the former choosing to retain many
English traditions from afternoon tea, cricket and the
monarch accepted (even by independent nations) as
head of the Commonwealth and are all symbolically
important. What the fall of the 'Imperial' Empire did

prompt was the reassessment of Britain's relationship with Europe. The 'Britain –Europe' debate begins where the previous chapter concluded – just after the Second World War.

After 1945 the Empire began to shrink. By the end of the next decade, strong arguments began to emerge both for and against Britain going into Europe. From the late 1950s the questions surrounding the survival of Britain's independence, her monarch and even her very identity began to hit mainstream. This is a Europe where from the late sixteenth century to the middle of the twentieth century Britain engaged within an extensive succession of military conflicts to protect the Channel and its trading routes (against the Spanish in 1588, the French in 1688 and again in 1793 against Napoleon's revolutionary France, Germany and the Kaiser in 1914 and more recently, Hitler's Third Reich). A (legitimate) primary concern was Britain's retention of the right to act in the best interests of her realm including total independence. The deteriorating economic situation eroded these concerns, voices from the right were ignored by parliamentary politicians who voted by a small majority for Britain to sign the Treaty of Rome. The treaty's ideological ambition was to create a single economic area void of internal barriers, providing total freedom of movement for its members, providing common domestic policies which would gradually integrate a common monetary system. Ultimately perhaps, to end all war between European states and discretely consolidate power. On 22 January 1972, Edward Heath the British Prime Minister signed on the dotted line and consequently on the 1 January 1973, Great Britain became historically part of the European

Community. It would be fair to claim, however, that Britain's unification with Europe, until now, has been largely felt a half-hearted commitment; a view shared by Europeans and Britons alike. Before signing the treaty, many resisted any form of solid European alignment, arguing that Britain's Commonwealth is there to trade with and should be given paramount priority with Britain historically always being strong enough to 'brave out the consequences' of any European threat.

The view of English purists has not changed in a hundred years and still carries enormous weight, at least in our subconscious. Anthony Sampson once claimed that whatever 'the geographical or ethnographical links' it is naïve to pretend 'that Britain is part of the continent. In nearly every field...the contrast stands out; in the strength and bloody-mindedness of her Unions, in the muddle of her car industry, in the outspokenness of her television, in the range of her newspapers, in her two party system, in the autonomy of her universities...in all these departments Britain sticks out as the odd-man-out of Europe, as clearly as driving on the left'. Our ancestors, as described at the beginning of this book, came from northern Europe in the form of Anglo-Saxons and Vikings, yet what took place during the amalgamation of these cultures on this island more than a thousand years ago, became something other than European. L.S.Amery, a British delegate once succinctly warned:

> It would run clean counter to the interests of Pan-Europe as well as to those of Great Britain if she were to accept membership of any form of European Union...Our hearts are not in Europe;

we would never share the truly European point of view nor become real patriots of Europe. Besides, we could never give up our own patriotism for an Empire which extends to all parts of the world – not even for a great ideal like that of Pan-Europe...We cannot belong at one and the same time to Pan-Europe and Pax-Britania, and no Briton, whatever his political party, would hesitate even for a second if faced with the choice between these two alternatives...The character of the British people makes it impossible for us to take part seriously in any Pan-European system.

The empire has now gone and recent economic arguments would challenge these ideas, but Amery's words here resonate with a spine-tingling truth about the disconnection between European and British identity. The confiscation of fertile British fishing territories, irresponsible unmitigated immigration and the tightening economic and fiscal pressures backed up by centuries of intense hostility and warfare does not advertise well for a sincere Union between Europe and Britain. The question here is; can we move past the scars of history, should we attempt to change our reticence, do we really want to?

One must consider the opposite voice, the other end of the scale (traditionally consisting mostly of Liberals), amidst the British ranks there are people very eager to adopt popular foreign policies in pursuit of fairer conditions at home. Policies backed by an International Court of Law, and such pro-Europeans align themselves with the tradition of the League of Nations. Suspiciously, our alleged 'friends' the United States of America, at every opportunity, encourages Britain's participation in the federalisation of Europe. In February 1945, when Churchill met with Roosevelt and Stalin, the issue of a new Europe dominated discussions then. Many Americans and particularly Roosevelt were extremely suspicious of Churchill and the British, suspecting our ambition to revive British imperial interests and restore Britain's former world power status. It should be mentioned that the dissolution of the British Empire was greatly beneficial and of the upmost interest to America. On the other hand, Britain has its fair share of European supporters from within. If a referendum was called now, various polls suggest, again, as in 1972, a small majority would vote in favour of a stronger Union with Europe. How accurate these polls are remains to be seen and are challenged by recent surveys.

Edwin Jones might wish to reduce England's history to a 'myth', yet every myth is founded on elements of truth. *The English Nation* is clearly influenced by the John Lingard and Herbert Butterfield pro-European camp, a school of thought which defined itself against the great scholarship of Lord Macaulay (1800-1859) and Sir G.M Trevelyan (1876-1962). Its idea of 'a new vision of Europe, united again by a system of common values' looks a long way from convincing the Spanish, Italian and Greek nations, let alone England. England is not the only nation with reservations either; the Scandinavian countries remain cautious over the increasing federalisation of Europe. A TNS survey carried out in 2012 on behalf of the European Commission, revealed that, for the European Union in its entirety, those who believe that their nation's interests are served in the EU are now in a minority at 42%. Those with a positive view of the EU are down from 52% in 2007 to 31% in May 2012. Polls have also recently indicated that about 31% of EU citizens trust the European Union as an institution, and about 60% do not trust the EU. Trust in the EU generally has fallen from 57% in 2007 to 31% in 2012 with the United Kingdom being the most skeptical with revealing figures of 16% trust, 75% distrust and the remainder unsure.

An interesting fact about the European Commission is that the Commissioners are not elected like the other members of the European Parliament; they are selected by the President of the EU who has been chosen by the preceding members and ratified by the Parliament. Comprehensive rules used to implement agreed EU policies are frequently made by the European Commission after consulting Member States. Thus in a more simplified explanation, EU Commissioners are neither voted in nor voted out. They spend their time concocting three main types of EU legislation which are – regulations (these are directly relevant in all Member States and are binding), directives (these are mandatory for Member States but they decide how they should be instigated in order to achieve the required outcome) and decisions (these are also binding on whom they are directed to and can include organisations as well as Member States).

Let's look at the main economic advantages and disadvantages of a greater Union with Europe. In the Euro, you cannot devalue if your currency becomes uncompetitive. This has been and remains a significant problem for Euro countries like Italy, Spain and Greece. By contrast, Britain has been able to devalue, reestablishing our competitiveness and allowing our economy more flexibility to ride through tough economic periods. In the Eurozone, interest rates are fixed by the ECB for the whole Euro region. However, this monetary policy could be detrimental for the UK economy. In 2008, London was hit hard by the financial crisis and was able to respond by the Bank of England cutting interest rates very quickly. In addition, the Bank of England was able to pursue 'quantitative easing' to try and stimulate economic growth. If we had fully committed to the Euro (as many at home are pursuing and many abroad desire) this would not have been possible. Thus it remains a valid argument that the UK recession of 2008 to the present would have been far more serious and even deeper without our independent monetary policy. Some perks of joining Europe fully, however, would include lower transaction costs for tourists and trading organisations, protection against exchange rate vacillations which would help exporters to know future costs and incomes. A potent advantage of joining the Euro is the reduction in exchange rate volatility with our main EU trading partners. Yet since 2003 the pound has displayed surprisingly very little exchange rate volatility. Joining the Euro would give the UK gains in terms of lower transaction costs and greater exchange rate stability but one must stress that for many businesses, these costs are a small percentage of total expenditures. Perhaps above all though, Britain would be at the heart of the Eurozone wielding greater influence over policy making across Europe. It can be argued that the debate over Britain's integration within Europe is not economic or financial at all, but for those who persist that this is the case then membership of the

Euro could potentially have very serious consequences, significantly for Britain, and even increase the risk of deflation and recession fueling our existing debt crisis. These potential complications surely far outweigh the trivial benefits of joining.

With national debts on the increase, unemployment queues stretching round the street corner and poverty on the rise, the European project across much of the EU has brought nothing but a downward spiral of economic misery. This is the current lived reality of the great European Project. Weighty European countries stand on the brink of financial collapse falling victim to the EU's continuous cycle of borrowing and bailouts while suffering the slow erosion of their social fabric and national independence. The ugly truth is that the single currency has facilitated the crisis by forcing interest rates down to figures that were totally unsustainable for numerous economies, especially Greece, Spain, Portugal and Ireland. The European Commission in many ways can be seen as abandoning any sense of financial reality. Thus, to gaze behind the pro-European spiel, we are to discover that the Eurozone was not an economic policy at all, but an insidious political strategy to attain absolute unification and integration at the expense of individual cultural identities. One should beware of being bullied into thinking we can only trade with Europe, or if England came out of Europe our trading relationship would deteriorate or cease altogether. This is economic nonsense. It is ideological and not financial factors that have dragged Britain aboard this sinking ship.

This discourse is a side issue, though related to the question of English identity. The result of General de Gaulle's outright rejection of Britain's first application to join what was then called the EEC (European Economic Community) back in 1963, was a reinvigoration of anti-French feeling throughout the sixties. De Gaulle then rejected Britain's second application to join in 1966-67 and is understood to have said that you cannot have 'two cocks living in one farmyard with ten hens'. By the end of 1968, however, his anti-Anglo-Saxon attitudes began to shake as France's gold reserves plummeted from 7 billion to 2 billion dollars. The five other members of the EEC expressed interest in Britain joining and displayed outward disagreement to French policy over Britain. As De Gaulle resigned in 1969, Pompidou took over as French President who had several pro-British cabinet members who advocated it is in the interests of France that Britain joins. The old rivalry between England and France far outdates de Gaulle, going back centuries, England owing plenty to France in its contribution to forming a concrete identity.

As the Anglo-French relationship has been so pivotal in shaping English identity, let us probe the depths of one of the world's most durable adversarial binary. The 130 year period between 1689 and 1815, was in many ways, a second hundred years war with France. Even long before this period, before the first hundred years war, the idea of France as a threat traces to the Norman Conquest of 1066. The French language never caught on in England. Firstly, this was never William's intention, and secondly, the Anglo-Saxons always remained bitter enemies of the Franks. Centuries later, France constantly posing as a hostile enemy, contributed to Britons uniting under one banner – the United Kingdom. For centuries we had a natural resistance to importing French manufactured goods and adopting too many French lexicons into the already rich English language. Conflicts between the two nearly always stemmed from competing for trade and commerce and the disputes over territories, which led to the Nine Years war and the Seven Years war (both won by Britain who reaped the profits from new markets as more and more colonies were engulfed in red and white). Such profits were all the more welcomed as they were taken from Britain's main competitor – France. The seven Years War could likely be seen as the most successful war Britain ever fought, resulting in the French losing many of their West African and West Indian territories and Britain conquering Canada. British imperialism expanded like no other in history, in such a short space of time. France struggled to compete with its sheer aggression, tenacity and affluence. Even then, in 1763 at the Treaty of Paris, Britain gave France back some of her recently acquired possessions. When it comes to identity, success goes a long way, particularly success in war. Wars against Revolutionary Napoleonic France, the Nine Years War, the Seven Years War and the War of Spanish succession, all produced spectacular military victories of a colossal magnitude for Britain, huge in terms of gaining trade routes and acquiring colonies. It should be remembered that, since the Union of the British Isles, Britain has never lost a war, with the exception of losing America. Even then, it was largely British fighting British, not Europeans fighting English.

This rapid expansion was in the end unsustainable for Britain to manage. Rapaciously over-inflating claiming authority over vast territories, Britain over-stretched herself with the largest empire the world had ever known; and consequently set herself up to fail. France of course has always done everything it can to facilitate

Britain's demise. The confrontation France has always provided has united English, Scottish, Irish and Welsh alike in the face of a common enemy. This has reinforced a marked sense of difference, supported by Britain being an island – the Channel demarcating a natural frontier, keeping the British enclosed together and preventing enemies from walking in. Anglo-French rivalry also and perhaps more deeply, takes on a religious dimension. Henry VIII's Reformation of the English Church, followed by Oliver Cromwell's vigorous protestant influence during the Revolution, marks the single most significant dividing point between England and mainland Europe. England and Britain have constantly been at war with Catholic France and her Papal friends in Spain, Germany and Italy. From 1682 to 1829, British Catholics were not appointed in state offices or Parliament and were denied the right to vote. They were highly discriminated against in terms of tax, education and rights to practice Catholicism. In times of war, Catholics would suffer abuse as the French enemy was always Catholic. France attempted to deport its Protestant population in 1685 and many of these refugees came to England.

There is a sense that Britons felt, in light of their unparalleled success, that they were, in some way protected by God and that it was their birthright to struggle against the 'anti-Christ'. The belief that 'under providence they would secure deliverance' insured superiority over Catholic peoples, particularly the French. Linda Colley transmits this perfectly when she states:

William Hogarth's brilliant *Calais Gate, or the Roast Beef of Old England* shows just how

savage this complacency could be, and just
how much it was relied upon to define and
demean the enemy. The fat monk salivating
over a newly roasted joint of imported English
beef; the singularly unattractive nuns, bare-
footed and fatuously pleased because they think
they have found Christ's image in the features
of a skate fish; the French soldiers, at once
scrawny and ragged and curiously effeminate;
even the forlorn Scottish Highlander, forced into
exile and garlic-eating because he has rebelled
against his Protestant Sovereign George II ... are
all centuries-old Protestant stereotypes.

This particular way of perceiving France was a way of
masking a deep sense of insecurity we harboured
towards French 'military capabilities and cultural
splendour'. England particularly felt that it was the first
nation to break away from the control of the Vatican,
becoming independent from Popish influence and
establishing its own independent church – The Church
of England. Although religion has far less influence on
modern England and its language today, our Protestant
roots are still ingrained very much in England's
perception of itself and others. One only has to look at
our national anthem (the term national anthem being
invented by the British):

God save our noble Queen
Long live our gracious Queen,
God save our Queen.

Look at William Blake's words of 'Jerusalem':

> Bring me my bow of burning gold:
> Bring me my arrows of desire:
> Bring me my spear: O clouds unfold
> Bring me my Chariot of fire
> I will not cease from Mental Fight
> Nor shall my sword sleep in my hand:
> Till we have built Jerusalem,
> In England's green and pleasant land.

The constant references to 'God', 'Jerusalem' and divine grace are quite telling symbols of identity, which we all sing to this day. Protestantism and its aggressive and suspicious outlook towards the world has left its mark within the English framework of patriotic identity. Catholic France, and to a lesser extent Spain, Italy and Germany have always represented the antithesis of England. The Anti-gallican Association founded during the war with France in 1748 was primarily designed to prevent any French imports into England, and to propagate all things English. In Charlton, South London, there is still a pub called the Anti-gallican. A ship called the 'Anti-Gallican' also sailed from Deptford in 1756. The thought of importing Frogs' legs and snails for domestic consumption would turn John Bull in his grave. The feeling in France is mutual.

Wars with France have always been more profitable than with Germany. England has often come out with extra colonies and bumper trade deals on the back of French defeats, however, with Germany, though not losing; England has more often than not been left worn out and impoverished as a result. The post war empire included Quebec with its 80,000 French Catholic population as well as large parts of Asia and India which were neither Christian nor White, contributing to England's identity with a growing sense of difference. Closer to home though, historically, English identity has a third important player (particularly now): that of Scotland. There were some reservations over the Union between Scotland and England on both sides of Hadrian's Wall. The Scots suspiciously felt that hundreds of years of hard earned independence were simply given up in unifying with England, the English cynically expressing that their poorer Scottish cousins would enjoy far more benefits from a Union. In other words, England was reassuming control of Scotland and Scotland would sponge off English assets and have access to its bountiful resources. These views, however, were in the minority but significant English numbers did not take too kindly to giving up 'English' for 'British'. Equally, Scotland was viewed as condemning the Union when it suited them but demanding (disproportionately) equal status with England inside it. Petty domestic squabbles aside, threats from hostile nations beyond our island posed a far greater threat, in many ways, rendering England and Scotland neither in complete cultural harmony with each other nor culturally distinguished and separate from one another. They came together in mutual interest to defend the British Isles.

Wars with Europe have probably ended. With Britain's main source of threat no longer present, people on both sides of the border are wondering what real benefits a United Kingdom brings. No longer bound in adversity, there are growing pressures from national discourses encouraging new sought after independence, particularly from Scotland; headed by Alex Salmond of the SNP, setting in motion a Scottish referendum on independence from the United Kingdom in 2014. Interestingly, the Scottish right wing is also talking of developing an intimate relationship with the EU, should independence capture the majority vote. Currently, the Scottish electorate seem very much divided on the question of independence, but the ramifications are obvious; should Scotland break away from the Union after three hundred years. It would be fair to say that the English perspective is mixed. Some display regret and suggest a negative impact on Great Britain, others express a sense of 'dropping baggage' leading to less pressure on English resources and a 'good riddance' attitude. Many are left feeling indifferent. In terms of identity, Scotland has flourished under the United Kingdom, England has not. English identity stands to gain far more with Scottish independence than Scottish identity. From the Anglo-Saxon times, England has prided itself on being a self-reliant, efficient, and driven race opposed to its Celtic fringes. It would be easier to state 'we are all the same', English, Scottish, Welsh and Irish – 'all from the same stock' and such debates are futile. Yet history tells us, though often composed of a mixture of all the tribes, we are not the same. Anglophobia and Scottophobia is an ancient and traditional antipathy premised on mutual hatred and mistrust. A deep history of armed conflict, invasions from both sides, pillaging, rape and slaughter has been kept alive in folklore... 'Bravehearts' against 'Lionhearts'. 'The Flower of Scotland' (the Scottish National anthem) explicitly feeds off the emotions of English Aggression with lyrics such as 'And stood against him, Proud Edward's army, and sent him homeward, ta think again'. One might go as far as saying Scottish identity is completely constructed around its hated and bitter rivalry with England. Strong words but with a degree of accuracy nonetheless. Wales and Ireland almost certainly harbour similar feelings. Consequently, Scotland, Ireland and Wales have always been conceived as adversarial territory, and in terms of civility the English are often reminded of the deep divisions in these parts with outward displays of Anglophobia. These archaic feelings go back to the forging of England during Anglo-Saxon times.

The English often feel, even today, that the House of Commons has a disproportionate representation of Scottish MP's to their population ratio and economic weight. Recent governments have had numerous Scottish cabinet ministers, particularly under New Labour. Such a Scottish presence has left English people feeling that the Scots have infiltrated English politics excessively and correlate this with the discouragement of any English patriotism most vehemently felt under Tony Blair and Gordon Brown. At one point in the very recent past, people were encouraged not to fly the St George's flag through fear of antagonising or offending minorities. Equally the topic of immigration has been supressed and ignored rendering it a taboo subject. These are a few examples which reside in the modern English mind. The belated reaction is manifesting itself in a wave of UKIP support at recent by-elections. Perhaps the UKIP vote is, in part, a protest vote, but it no longer just applies to Europe. We may be starting to see more evidence that the populations of Great Britain are increasingly more conscious of their internal divisions as there no longer exists an obligation to fight together against a common enemy. A typically cynical view of the break-up of the United Kingdom would be to presume that France and many others in Europe would rub their hands with exuberant glee at the thought of a dismantling Britain. It seems clear that Britain has been weakened by fighting above its weight for a long period of time; exhausted physically, mentally and economically after the last war, Britain simply did not have the energy, resources or manpower to hold on to its vast empire. As Sir Henry Tizard once said: 'We are a great nation, but if we continue to behave like a great power we shall soon cease to be a great nation'. The premise appears to hold true, that we are greater as a unification of all the kingdoms of Great Britain. Its gradual demise might well be our fault for not readjusting to a 'British' identity, and for clinging on to our specific regional affiliations.

After World War Two, when the project of a European Union was heating up, Britain showed outward condescension towards European countries, loosely based on anxieties surrounding any compromise of British independence. This was fuelled by a very over-confident Britain – the only European nation to have emerged victorious in the Great War. Churchill himself spoke highly of a 'United Europe' but the small print of his policies suggested in a very subtle way, that a European unification did not necessarily embrace full British involvement. As Peter Clarke reveals:

> Declining its opportunities to shape the new Europe, the British Government persistently looked to a world role. This explains the decision

to build a British atomic bomb; that Britain was capable of doing this in turn flattered pretensions to global influence. The development of a nuclear capability, under the leadership of the brilliant mathematician William Penney, and without the benefit of US cooperation, was certainly a tribute to the high calibre of British scientific expertise in nuclear physics.

There were of course other reasons for Britain's inertia. After hundreds of years of pence, shillings and farthings, the old imperial system was replaced and made redundant by the European metrication system – a system originating from Napoleonic influence – symbolic, to Brits, of a victory for France, as once where a third of the earth under British rule used stones, pounds and ounces were now forced to adopt French grams and kilograms. The decimalisation of sterling in 1971 forced school children to reconfigure their analytical skills when considering weights, dimensions and distances. The anti-Europe feelings are inextricably linked to the symbolism of the fall of empire, and to the realisation that in joining Europe like all the rest, Britain was to lose its special status.

The problem may well be that Britain, or particularly England, is not genuinely European. This is evident whenever important international issues occur, as our reaction instinctively seems to be detached from Europe's. English nationalism has perhaps been constructed differently over the centuries, an identity defined by three major elements: its protestant disposition explaining a shared anti-Catholic mentality, historical victories against Spain, Germany and France in which it took (and still takes) a great shared sense of pride and finally the remnants of its vast empire. It is difficult to contest that all these factors are losing potency by the day. The English folk memory is so deeply embedded that it has separated England from mainland Europe from way before the forging of Great Britain or even before the rise of the empire. Splendid and unique in our isolation, we consistently feel we owe nothing and borrow nothing of any relevance or importance from Europe. Professor David Knowles describes a 'certain blend of qualities that is peculiarly English, and that throughout the ages...has been embodied again and again in great Englishmen'. Among those Englishmen he quotes Alfred the Great, Thomas More, Venerable Bede, Chaucer and Shakespeare, and included qualities such as loyalty, trust, tenacity, warm-heartedness, simplicity, seriousness, sanity and a keen sense of pathos combined with a bull-dog spirit of courage as accurately portraying the strengths of character of the English. Affected by the remarkable successes of war, a streak of irrational xenophobia undermines these qualities but manifests itself as a kind of side effect from a history of outward aggression England is always and has always been faced with. Europe is full of war-like people, fiercely territorial, and England rose to the top of these fighting nations reaching its peak in the early twentieth century.

Britain is the most reluctant of all the large European nations to merge with her neighbours. The construction of the Channel Tunnel did not really have the impact that was desired – a physical connection with the mainland. Our reluctance, in the spirit of total honesty, may stem from the unwilling acknowledgement that our greatest years are now behind us and that we are now just another European country. There is also the matter of not easily giving up over a thousand years of sovereign independence and self-reliance. Joining a group of peoples who have systematically attempted to take this away from Britain was always going to be a tall order. For European nations to say they have not been envious of England's position would be a blatant misconception. Though never acknowledged, repetitive attempts have continuously been made to undermine Britain, and her amalgamation with Europe is often perceived as another ploy to further diminish the fading greatness of Britain. The French naturally like to dismiss such ideas as 'de propagande nationaliste et xenophobe'. Yet it is true that European regulations such as the CAP have caused incalculable damage to British farming and fishing industries, and, being left with a growing inability to legislate ourselves, we are unable to deport known terrorists such as Abu Qatada because of the European Courts. There is no xenophobia in the mathematics which tell us that Europe has harmed Britain's economic competitiveness, not enhanced it. 'Membership of the EU is a retrograde step for industry that militates against efficiency, competitiveness, progress and development'.

There has also been an ideological link with the rise of Darwinism, enforcing a powerful Teutonic myth that England's advancement represented stages of natural evolutionary progress by originating from a particular group of people. Charles Darwin's *Origin of Species* in 1859 strengthened nationalist ideas at the common and political level. From its alleged superior qualities of character deriving from the biologically superior German stock, Englishness somehow embodied all the greatness of the northern European bloodlines to become a successful race, consistently evidenced in its victories in all wars. However fabricated and fairy tale this notion is, there remains an unnatural sense of superiority over other Europeans culminating in many clever and thoughtful ways of justifying it. 'Survival of the fittest' is an outdated and backward explanation of England's unique rise as a group of people who largely originate back to the old German forest communities. Ideas of England's progress and enlightenment are better articulated and gloriously enforced by the moving rhetoric found in S. Turner's *The History of England*:

> Happy are the aged, who cannot depart without the exhilarating view of this interesting aspect; and who had the satisfaction of witnessing its progressive growth, and of knowing that it has not been the scheme or usurpation of any turbulent ambition. It has been the grand evolution of the providential destiny of our country, produced by no human contrivance or vicious rapacity. England has been impelled by causes, not originating from herself, to become what she is; and as long as she exercises her sovereignty to promote the peace, improvements, the morality, the religion, and the happiness of mankind, so long will her aggrandisement be continued, until some other nations arise, if any ever shall, whose superior predominance will still more signally advance the future progress of our emulous, exited, and never-resting order if intellectual being. Nations

and cabinets may plan and battle but...At present, the BRITISH dominion appears to be transcended by no other, in the diffusion of these blessings.

Although more relevant to previous centuries, our national identity draws its strength from our historical achievements, where the chariot wheels of English imperialism rotated more efficiently and successfully than all others before it.

As we move ever swiftly through the twenty-first century, time indiscriminately swallowing up the years, England is faced with a myriad of questions with one shining more brightly than all the rest. Is it going to integrate with Europe, or not? There are economic arguments for and against, there are political reasons for and against, however, the overriding issue is one of identity and how we see ourselves. It was overheard recently that 'sovereignty is absolute or nothing'. England has always been partly defined by its enemies. In this context, her identity is safe as her adversarial list is as prevalent today as it was two hundred years ago. The difference is, England and her Commonwealth now stand alone; and as Churchill always said 'alone if necessary' we will go on to the end. I cannot think of a poem which resonates with such personal feelings in describing one's affection for their homeland, so acutely in tune with the affinity to a nation than the all inspiring English poet William Ernest Henley and his great (if not the greatest) Victorian poem of the age. If nations could speak, this is England's testament. This poem truly embodies the English soul and we should take it with us, into a threatening future fraught with challenges on a titanic scale, and adopt such lyrics into a song of England – a timeless England. A Lionheart Nation.

Out of the night that covers me,
Black as the Pit from pole to pole,
I thank whatever gods may be
For my unconquerable soul.

In the fell clutch of circumstance
I have not winced nor cried aloud.
Under the bludgeonings of chance
My head is bloody, but unbowed.

Beyond this place of wrath and tears
Looms but the Horror of the shade,
And yet the menace of the years
Finds, and shall find, me unafraid.

It matters not how strait the gate,
How charged with punishments the scroll.
I am the master of my fate:
I am the captain of my soul.

Bibliography

General

Clarke. P, 1996, *Hope and Glory: Britain 1900-1990*, The Penguin Press, London

Colley, L, 2005, *Britons: Forging the Nation 1707-1837*, Yale University Press, U.S, Reading

Davis, R.H.C, 1970, *A History of Medieval Europe: From Constantine to Saint Louis*, Longman Group, Essex, New York

Douglas. D.C, (Editor) 1996, *English Historical Documents*: Volume 4, Eyre and Spottiswoode, London, Edinburgh

Hamerow. H, 2002, *Early Medieval Settlements*, Oxford University Press, Oxford, New York

Holmes. G, (Editor) 1988, *The Oxford Illustrated History of Medieval Europe*, Oxford University Press, Oxford, New York

Jones. E, 2000, *The English Nation: The Great Myth*, Sutton Publishing Ltd, Gloucestershire

Koenigsberger. H. G, 1987, *Medieval Europe 400-1500*, Longman Group, Essex, New York

Schwarz. B, (Editor) 1996, *The Expansion of England: Race, Ethnicity and Cultural History*, Routledge, London, New York

Teed. P, 1976, *The Move to Europe: Britain 1880-1972*, Hutchinson and Co, London

Walder. D, (Editor) 1990, *Literature in the Modern World*, Oxford University Press, Oxford, New York

McKie. R, 2006, *Face of Britain*, Simon & Schuster UK Ltd, Australia, Syndney

Henry V

Allmand. C.T, 1976, War, Literature and Politics in the Late Medieval Ages, Liverpool University Press

Baker. G. L, 1889, Chronicon Galfridi le Baker de Svynebroke (Edited by E.M.Thompson), Oxford

Bennett. H.S, 1947, Chaucer and the Fifteenth Century

Burne. A.H, 1955, The Crecy War. A Military History of the Hundred Years War From 1337 to the Peace of Bretigny 1360, Eyre & Spottiswoode

Earle. P, 1972, The Life and Times of Henry V, George Weidenfield & Nicolson Ltd, UK

Elmham. T, 1850, Henrici Quinti Angliae Regis Gesta, English Historical Society, London

Eyre & Spottiswoode, 1956, The Agincourt War: A Military History of the Battles of the Hundred Years War From 1369-1453

Froissart, Chronicles – trans. By Lord Berners

Green. V.H.H, 1955, The Later Plantagenets

Holmes. G, 1962, The Later Middle Ages 1272-1485, Thomas Nelson & Sons Ltd, London

Jacob. E.F, 1961, The Fifteenth Century 1399-1485, Oxford Clarendon Press, Oxford

Keen. M.H, 1973, England in the Later Middle Ages

Lander. J.R, 1969, Conflict and Stability in Fifteenth Century England, Hutchinson University Library, London

Lodge. E.C, 1926, Gascony Under English Rule, Methuen

McFarlane. K.B, 1973, The Nobility of Later Medieval England, Oxford University Press, Oxford

Newhall. R.A, 1921, English Historical Review: The War Finances of Henry V and the Duke of Bedford

Seward. D, 2003, A Brief History of the Hundred Years War, Robinson, London

Thomson. J.A.F, 1983, The Transformation of Medieval England: 1370-1529, Longman Group UK, Essex

Wilkinson. B, 1948, Constitutional History of Medieval England - extracts taken

Wycliffe, Select English Writings – Edited by H.E Winn

Oliver Cromwell

Bennett. M, 1995, The English Civil War, Longman Group Ltd, Harlow, Essex

Braddick. M, 2008, God's Fury, England's Fire- A New History of the English Civil Wars, Penguin Group, London

Brett. R.S, 1958, Oliver Cromwell, Adam & Charles Black, London

Calvin. J, 1949, The Institutes of the Christian Religion – trans. By H Beviridge

Davies. G, 1959 (Second Ed), The Early Stuarts, Oxford University Press, Oxford

Davies-Langdon. J, 1966, A Collection of Contemporary Documents, Jacksaw Publications Ltd, UK

Elton. G.R, 1976, Renaissance and Reformation 1300-1648 – Third Edition, Macmillan, New York

Firth. C, 1900, Oliver Cromwell and the Rule of the Puritans in England, Oxford University Press, Oxford

Fraser. A, 1973, Cromwell: Our Chief of Men, Cox & Wyman Ltd, London

Gardiner. S.R, 1987, History of the Great Civil War, Longmans, Green & Co, Windrush Press, London – Volume 1,2,3

Gregg. P, 1967, The Levellers and the English Revolution, Brailsford

Hill. C, 1970, God's Englishmen: Oliver Cromwell and the English Revolution, Willmer Brothers Ltd, Great Britain

Miller. C.F.P, 1938, The Puritans, New York

Morrill. J, 1992, Revolution and Restoration: England in the 1650s, Collins & Brown, London

Seel. G.E, 1999, The English Wars and Republic 1637-1660, Routledge, London

Sharp. J.A, 1987, Early Modern England, A Social History 1550-1760, Edward Arnold, Great Britain

Sommerville. J.P, 1999, Royalists and Patriots – Politics and Ideology in England 1603-1640, Pearson Education Limited, Harlow, Essex

Winston Churchill

Addison. P, 2005, Churchill: The Unexpected Hero, Oxford

Churchill. W.S, 1931, My Early Life, Thornton Butterworth, London

Churchill. W.S, 1938, The Malakand Field Force, Longmans & Co, London

Hastings. M, 1984, Overlord: D Day and the Battle For Normandy 1944, London

Heinmann, 1976, Winston S Churchill, Vol VI: Their Finest Hour, 1939-41, London

Heinmann, 1983, Winston S Churchill, Vol VII: The Road to Victory, 1941-45, London

Jenkins. R, 2001, Churchill, MacMillan, London

Keegan. J, 2003, Churchill, Phoenix, London

Lamb. R, 1991, Churchill As War Leader, Weidenfield & Nicolson, London

Murray. W, 1984, The Change in the European Balance of Power 1938-39, Princeton University Press

Taylor. A.J.P, 1961, The Origins of the Second World War, Hamish Hamilton, London